Closer

'Throughout *Closer*, his second play, Patrick Marber writes like a master. On the surface, *Closer* is brisk, urbane, witty, obscene, modern, quotable, slick; beneath the skin, it is deeply felt, painful, sad, and wise ... It is about sexual jealousy and sexual desire; and it is keenly alert to human isolation even within intense relationships ... It is the best new play the National has presented since Marber's first play, *Dealer's Choice* ... Marber seems to me to have the most assured sense for dramatic rhythm of any English playwright to have emerged since Pinter.' *Financial Times*

'What I love most about Marber's writing here is that he gets right down to what Yeats described as "the foul rag-and-bone shop of the heart". Anyone who has loved and lost, anyone who has experienced infidelity or felt love die, will watch this play with stomach churning pangs of recognition ... the writing seems to have been ripped straight from the gut. In contrast, the construction has great formal beauty, consisting of a series of duologues which gradually move the action forward.... The sense of artistic control is formidable ... I'd be astonished if there's a better new play this year.'
Daily Telegraph

Patrick Marber was born in London. His first play, *Dealer's Choice*, premiered at the Royal National Theatre in February 1995. It won the *Evening Standard* Award for Best Comedy and the Writers' Guild Award for Best West End Play. *Closer*, his second play, premiered at the Royal National Theatre in May 1997 and won the *Evening Standard* Award for Best Comedy and the *Time Out* Award for Best West End Play in 1997. He has also written extensively for television and radio, including *After Miss Julie* (BBC Television, 1995).

by the same author

Dealer's Choice
After Miss Julie

for a complete catalogue of Methuen Drama write to:

Methuen Drama
Random House
20 Vauxhall Bridge Road
London SW1V 2SA

Patrick Marber

Closer

Methuen Drama

Methuen Modern Plays

3 5 7 9 10 8 6 4

First published in Great Britain in 1997
by Methuen
Random House, 20 Vauxhall Bridge Road, London SW1V 2SA

This revised edition published 1997

Random House Australia (Pty) Limited
20 Alfred Street, Milsons Point, Sydney,
New South Wales 2061, Australia

Random House New Zealand Limited
18 Poland Road, Glenfield,
Auckland 10, New Zealand

Random House South Africa (Pty) Limited
Endulini, 5A Jubilee Road, Parktown 2193, South Africa

Random House UK Limited Reg. No. 954009

Distributed in the United States of America
by Heinemann, a division of Reed Elsevier Inc.
361 Hanover Street, Portsmouth, New Hampshire NH 03901 3959

A CIP catalogue record for this book is available from the British Library

Papers used by Random House UK Limited are natural, recyclable
products made from wood grown in sustainable forests. The
manufacturing processes conform to the environmental regulations of the
country of origin.

ISBN 0 413 70950 7

Typeset by Deltatype Ltd, Birkenhead, Merseyside
Printed and bound in Great Britain by Cox & Wyman Ltd, Reading,
Berkshire

Caution

Closer

For Debra

Closer was first presented in the Cottesloe auditorium of the Royal National Theatre, London, on 22 May 1997. The cast was as follows:

Alice	Liza Walker
Dan	Clive Owen
Larry	Ciaran Hinds
Anna	Sally Dexter

Closer transferred to the Lyttleton auditorium of the Royal National Theatre, London, on 16 October 1997. The cast was as follows:

Alice	Liza Walker
Dan	Mark Strong
Larry	Neil Dudgeon
Anna	Sally Dexter

Directed by Patrick Marber
Designed by Vicki Mortimer
Lighting by Hugh Vanstone
Music by Paddy Cunneen
Sound by Simon Baker
Photography by Hugo Glendinning
Stage Manager Ernest Hall
Deputy Stage Manager Emma B. Lloyd
Assistant Stage Manager Paul Greaves

Characters

Alice, *a girl from the town. Early twenties.*
Dan, *a man from the suburbs. Thirties.*
Larry, *a man from the city. Late thirties/early forties.*
Anna, *a woman from the country. Mid-thirties.*

Setting

The play is set in London, 1993–1997.

Scene One: January 1993
Scene Two: June 1994
Scene Three: January 1995
Scene Four: January 1995
Scene Five: June 1995
Scene Six: June 1996
Scene Seven: September 1996
Scene Eight: October 1996
Scene Nine: November 1996
Scene Ten: December 1996
Scene Eleven: January 1997
Scene Twelve: June 1997

The above dates are for information only. They should not be included in any production programme or design.

All settings should be minimal.

Note

This revised version of *Closer* incorporates cuts, additions and rewrites effected in transferring the play from the Cottesloe to the Lyttelton. This version replaces that previously published and is the sole authorised version of the play.

An alternative 'spoken' version of Scene Three appears at the end of this text.

Act One

Scene One

Hospital.

Early morning.

Alice *is sitting. She is wearing a black coat. She has a rucksack by her side. Also a brown leather briefcase.*

She strikes a match, watches it burn, blows it out.

She rolls down one sock. She has a cut on her leg. Quite bloody. She looks at it. She picks some strands of wool from the wound.

She looks at the briefcase. Thinks. Looks around. Opens it. She searches inside. She pulls out some sandwiches in silver foil and a green apple. She opens the sandwiches and looks at the contents, smiles, puts them back. She shines the apple. She bites into it.

As she starts to chew **Dan** *enters. He wears a suit and an overcoat. He stops, watches her eating his apple. He is holding two hot drinks in styrofoam cups.*

Alice Sorry. I was looking for a cigarette.

Dan I've given up.

Dan *hands her a drink.*

Alice Have you got to be somewhere?

Dan Work. Didn't fancy my sandwiches?

Alice I don't eat fish.

Dan Why not?

Alice Fish piss in the sea.

Dan So do children.

Alice I don't eat children either. What's your work?

Dan Journalism.

Alice What sort?

Dan (*reluctant*) Obituaries.

Alice Do you like it . . . in the dying business?

Dan (*smiles*) It's a living.

Beat.

Alice Do you think a doctor will come?

Dan Eventually. Does it hurt?

Alice I'll live.

Dan Shall I put your leg up?

Alice Why?

Dan That's what people do in these situations.

Alice What is this 'situation'?

They look at each other.

Dan Do you want me to put your leg up?

Alice Yes, please.

He lifts her leg onto a chair.

Who cut off your crusts?

Dan Me.

Alice Did your mother cut off your crusts when you were a little boy?

Dan I believe she did, yes.

Alice You should eat your crusts.

Dan You should stop smoking.

He looks at her leg on the chair.

I've got a mobile, is there anyone you'd like to phone?

Alice I don't know anyone.

Beat.

Thank you for scraping me off the road.

Dan My pleasure.

Alice You knight.

Dan *looks at her.*

Dan You damsel.

Beat.

Why didn't you look?

Alice I never look where I'm going.

Dan I looked into your eyes and then you stepped into the road.

Alice Then what?

Dan You were lying on the ground, you focused on me, you said, 'Hallo, stranger.'

Alice What a slut.

Dan I noticed your leg was cut.

Alice Did you notice my legs?

Dan In what sense?

Alice In the sense, 'nice legs'?

Dan Quite possibly.

Alice Then what?

Dan The cabbie got out. He crossed himself. He said, 'Thank fuck, I thought I'd killed her.' I said, 'Let's get her to a hospital.' He hesitated, I think he thought there'd be paperwork and he'd be held responsible. So I said, with a slight sneer, 'Please, just drop us at the hospital.'

Alice Show me the sneer.

Dan *sneers.*

Alice   Very good.

Dan   We put you in the cab and came here.

Alice   What was I doing?

Dan   You were murmuring, 'I'm very sorry for all the inconvenience.' I had my arm round you . . . your head was on my shoulder.

Alice   Was my head . . . 'lolling'?

Dan   That's exactly what it was doing.

Pause.

Alice   You have the saddest looking bun I've ever seen. Can I have it?

Dan *opens his briefcase.*

Alice   You'll be late for work.

Dan   Are you saying you want me to go?

Alice   No.

She puts her hand in the briefcase.

Dan   You can have half.

She removes the bun, tears it in two and begins to eat.

Why were you at Blackfriars Bridge?

Alice   I'd been dancing at a club near Smithfield. Do you like dancing?

Dan   I'm too old.

Alice   Codswallop.

Dan   I'm too old to *jive* let alone 'rave' or whatever it's called this week.

Alice   How old are you?

Dan   Thirty-five.

Alice   Half-time?

Dan Thank you very much. So ...

Alice I went for a walk. I went to see the meat being unloaded.

Dan The carcasses?

Alice Yes.

Dan Why?

Alice Because they're repulsive. Then I found a tiny park ... it's a graveyard too. Postman's Park. Do you know it?

Dan No.

Alice There's a memorial to ordinary people who died saving the lives of others. It's most curious. Then I decided to go to Borough ... so I went to Blackfriars Bridge to cross the river.

Pause. **Dan** *offers her the other half of the bun.*

Alice Are you sure?

Dan Yeah, it's yesterday's sad bun.

Beat.

That park ... it's near here?

Alice Yes.

Dan Is there a statue?

Alice A Minotaur.

Dan Yeah, I do know it ... we sat there ... (my mother's dead) ... my father and I sat there the afternoon she died. She died here actually ... she was a smoker.

Remembering gradually.

My father ... ate ... an egg sandwich ... his hands shook with grief ... pieces of egg fell on the grass ... butter on his top lip ... but I don't remember ... a memorial.

Pause.

Alice   Is your father still alive?

Dan   Just. He's in a home.

Alice   How did you end up writing obituaries? What did you really want to be?

Pause.

Dan   Oh . . . I had dreams of being a writer but I had no voice – no talent. So . . . I ended up in the 'Siberia' of journalism.

Alice   Tell me what you do. I want to imagine you in Siberia.

Dan   Really?

Alice   Yes.

Dan   Well . . . we call it 'the obits page'. There's three of us; me, Harry and Graham. The first thing someone will say (usually Graham) is 'Who's on the slab?' Meaning did anyone important die overnight. Are you sure you want to know?

Alice   Yes.

Dan   If someone 'important' did die we go to the 'deep freeze' which is a computer containing all the obituaries and we'll find the dead person's life.

Alice   People's obituaries are already written when they're still alive?

Dan   Some people's. If no one important has died then Harry – he's the editor – decides who we lead with and we check facts, make calls, polish the prose. Some days I might be asked to deal with the widows or widowers. They try to persuade us to run an obituary of their husbands or wives. They feel we're dishonouring their loved ones if we don't . . . but . . . most of them are . . . well, there isn't the space. At six we stand round the computer and read the next day's page, make final changes, put in a few euphemisms to amuse ourselves . . .

Alice Such as?

Dan 'He was a clubbable fellow', meaning he was an alcoholic. 'He valued his privacy' – gay. 'He enjoyed his privacy' – raging queen. 'She was a convivial hostess' –

Alice A pissed old slapper?

Dan Exactly.

Pause. **Alice** *slowly strokes* **Dan***'s face. He is unnerved but not unwilling.*

Alice And what would your euphemism be . . .

Dan (*soft*) For me?

Alice Mmm.

Dan He was . . . 'reserved'.

Alice A lonely old bastard?

Dan Perhaps.

Alice And me?

Dan You were . . . 'disarming'.

Beat.

Alice How did you get this job?

Dan They ask you to write your own obituary. If it amuses, you're in.

They are close, looking at each other.
Larry *walks past in a white coat.* **Dan** *stops him.*

Dan Excuse me, we've been waiting quite a long time. Will someone come soon, do you think?

Larry I'm sorry, it's not my . . .

He is about to walk away. He looks briefly at **Alice***. Pretty girl. He stops.*

What happened?

Alice I was hit by a car.

Dan   She was unconscious for about ten seconds.

Larry   May I?

He gently puts her leg down.

You can feel your toes?

Alice   Yes.

Larry   What's this?

Alice   It's a scar.

Larry (*smiling*)   Yes, I know it's a scar. How did you get it?

Alice   In America. A truck.

Larry   Awful job.

Alice   I was in the middle of nowhere.

Larry   You'll be fine.

Alice   Can I have one?

Larry *looks at her.*

A cigarette . . .

She nods at his pocket. **Larry** *takes out his packet of cigarettes and hands her one.*

Larry   Don't smoke it here.

Dan   Thank you.

Larry *exits.*

Dan   What were you doing in the middle of nowhere?

Alice   Travelling.

Dan   Alone?

Alice   With . . . a male.

Dan   What happened to this . . . male?

Alice   I don't know, I ran away.

Dan Where?

Alice   New York.

Dan Just like that?

Alice   It's the only way to leave. 'I don't love you any more, goodbye.'

Dan Supposing you do still love them?

Alice   You don't leave.

Dan You've never left someone you still love?

Alice   No.

Pause.

Dan When did you come back?

Alice   Yesterday.

Dan Did you like New York?

Alice   Sure.

Dan Were you . . . studying?

Alice   Stripping.

Beat. **Alice** *smiles.*

Look at your little eyes.

Dan I can't see my little eyes.

Alice   They're popping out. You're a cartoon.

Dan Were you . . . 'good' at it?

Alice   Exceptional.

Dan Why?

Alice   I know what men want.

Dan Really?

Alice   Oh yes.

Dan Tell me . . .

Alice   Men want a girl who looks like a boy. They want to protect her but she must be a survivor. And she must come . . . like a train . . . but with elegance.

Beat.

What do *you* want?

Pause.

Dan   Who was this . . . male?

Alice   A punter. But once I was his he hated me stripping.

Dan *smiles.*

Alice   Do you have a girlfriend?

Dan (*grim*)   Ruth. What do *you* want?

Alice   To be loved.

Dan   That simple?

Alice   It's a big want.

Dan   Where are your . . . belongings?

She points to her rucksack.

Alice   I'm a waif. I appeal to your manly instincts?

Dan   Yes, you do.

Alice   You want to protect me from the ravages of the world?

Dan   Perhaps.

Alice   Join the queue, Buster. Anyway, you've got to see 'who's on the slab'.

Pause.

Dan   Will you meet me after work?

Alice   Sure. Why don't you take the day off. I'll call in for you and say you're sick.

Dan I can't.

Alice Yes you can. Don't be such a pussy.

Dan I might be anyone, I might be a psychotic.

Alice I've met psychotics, you're not.

Dan You might be.

Alice You know I'm not.

She growls.

Phone.

Dan *hands her his mobile.*

Dan Memory one.

She punches in the number.

Alice Who do I speak to?

Dan Harry Masters.

Alice What's your name?

Dan Mr Daniel Woolf. What's your name?

Alice Alice. My name is Alice Ayres.

Blackout.

Scene Two

Anna's *studio.*

Late afternoon.

Anna *stands behind her camera.* **Dan** *sits on a high stool.* **Anna** *takes a shot.*

Anna Good.

Dan What was this building?

Anna A refuge for fallen women.

Shot.

Dan   Wasn't there a river here?

Anna   The Fleet. They built over it in the eighteenth century.

Dan   A buried river.

Shot.

Anna   If you stand on Blackfriars Bridge you can see where it comes out.

Dan   I think I will.

Anna   You must.

Shot.

Stay there. It inspired an urban legend – a bit like the alligators in New York.

Shot.

People thought that pigs were breeding underground and then one day this big fat boar swam out into the Thames and trotted off along the Embankment.

Dan   So it was true?

Anna   No, it escaped from Smithfield.

Shot.

Dan   Pigs swim?

Anna   Surprisingly well.

Shot.

Relax.

Anna *changes film, adjusts a light, etc.*

Dan   Can I smoke?

Anna   Yeah.

She hands him an ashtray. **Dan** *lights a cigarette.*

I liked your book.

Dan   Thanks.

Alice   When's it published?

Dan   Next year, how come you read it?

Anna   Your publisher sent me a manuscript, I read it last night, you kept me up till four.

Dan   I'm flattered.

Anna   Is your anonymous heroine based on someone real?

Dan   She's . . . someone called Alice.

Anna   How does she feel about you stealing her life?

Dan   *Borrowing* her life. I'm dedicating the book to her. She's pleased.

He is staring at her. She turns, looks at him.

Dan   Do you exhibit?

Anna   Next summer.

Dan   Portraits?

Anna   Yes.

Dan   Of who?

Anna   Strangers.

Beat.

Dan   How do your strangers feel about *you* stealing their lives?

Anna   Borrowing. An image.

Dan   Am I a stranger?

Anna   No. You're a job.

Pause.

Dan   You're beautiful.

Anna   No I'm not.

She gestures for him to sit again. She looks into the camera.

Anna   Chin up, you're a sloucher.

Shot.

Dan   You didn't find it obscene, the book.

Anna   No, I thought it was honest.

Shot.

Dan   About what?

Anna   About sex. (*Correcting herself.*) About love.

Shot.

Dan   In what way?

Shot.

Anna   You wrote it.

Dan   But you read it.

He looks at her. She looks down the lens.

Anna   Don't raise your eyebrows, you look smug.

Shot.

Dan   But you did like it?

Anna   Yes, but I could go off it.

Shots. She unloads the film.

Dan   Any criticisms?

Anna   Bad title.

Dan   Got a better one?

Anna   Really?

Dan   Yes.

Anna   'The Aquarium'.

Dan   You liked that bit?

Anna   Yes . . .

Dan *approaches.*

Dan You like aquariums?

Anna Not especially ...

He strokes her arm.

Dan You should go to the one at London Zoo, you might change your mind ...

Anna I doubt it ...

Dan You might ...

He touches her face. They look at each other.

Anna I don't kiss strange men.

Dan Neither do I.

Anna Do you and this ... Alice ... live together?

Pause.

Dan Yes.

He continues to touch her.

Anna (*nods.*) 'She has one address in her address book; ours ... under "H" for home.'

Dan I've cut that line.

Anna Why?

Dan Too sentimental.

She gently pulls away from him.

Dan Are you married?

Anna Yes ... no ... yes ... separated.

Dan Do you have any children?

Anna No.

Dan Would you like some?

Anna Yes, but not today.

She turns off the lamp and begins to pack up her stuff. Session over.

Would Alice like children?

Dan   She's too young.

Anna   And does she really have no family?

Dan   She's got no one. Actually, she's coming to meet me here, quite soon.

Anna   Well, there you go. Why are you wasting her time?

Dan   I'm not. I'm grateful to her ... she's ... completely unleavable.

Anna   And you don't want someone else to get their dirty hands on her?

Dan   Maybe.

Anna   Men are crap.

Dan   But all the same ...

Anna   They're still crap.

The door buzzer goes.

Your muse.

Dan   (*ironic*)   You've ruined my life.

Anna   You'll get over it.

The door buzzer goes again. They look at each other.
Pause. **Dan** *exits to answer the door.* **Anna** *thinks, rueful.*

Dan *enters with* **Alice**. *Her hair is a different colour to Scene One.*

Dan   Alice ... Anna.

Anna   Hi.

Alice *looks at* **Anna**.

Alice   I'm sorry if you're still working.

Anna   No, we've just finished.

Beat.

Alice   Was he well-behaved?

Anna   Reasonably. Do you want some tea?

Alice   No thanks, I've been serving it all day. Is there
a . . . ?

Anna   Through there.

Alice *exits.*

Anna   *She* is beautiful.

Dan   Yes, she is. I've got to see you.

Anna   No.

Pause.

Dan   Why are you getting all . . . sisterly.

Anna   I'm not getting sisterly, I don't want trouble.

Dan   I'm not trouble.

Anna   You're taken.

Dan   I've got to see you.

Anna   Tough.

Pause. **Alice** *enters.*

Alice (*To* **Anna**.)   Will you take my photo? I've never
been photographed by a professional before. I can pay you.

Pause.

Anna   No . . . I'd like to.

Alice (*to* **Dan**)   Only if you don't mind.

Dan   Why should I?

Alice   Because you'll have to go away. (*To* **Anna**.) We
don't want *him* here while we're working, do we?

Beat.

Dan   I'll wait in the pub on the corner.

He kisses **Alice**.

Have fun. (*To* **Anna**.) Thank you. Good luck with your exhibition.

Anna   Good luck with your book.

Dan   Thanks.

Dan *exits*.

Alice   You've got an exhibition?

Anna   Only a small one. Take a seat.

Alice *sits*. **Anna** *busies herself with the camera*, **Alice** *watches her*.

Anna   I read Dan's book. You've had ... quite a life.

Alice   Thanks.

Beat.

Alice   Are you single?

Anna   Yes ...

Alice   Who was your last boyfriend?

Anna   My husband.

Alice   What happened to him?

Beat. **Anna** *unsure where this is leading.*

Anna   Someone younger ...

Alice   What did he do?

Anna   He made money. In the City.

Alice   We used to get those in the clubs. Wall Street boys.

Anna   So ... these places were quite ... up-market?

Alice   Some of them. But I preferred the dives.

Anna   Why?

Alice The poor are more generous.

Pause. **Anna** *looks back into the camera.*

Anna You've got a great face. How do you feel about Dan using your life, for his book?

Alice None of your fucking business.

Pause.

Anna Sorry . . .

Pause.

Alice When he let me in downstairs he had . . . this . . . look. I listened to your . . . conversation.

Silence.

Anna I don't know what to say.

Alice Take my picture.

Beat.

Anna I'm not a thief, Alice.

Anna *focuses her camera.*

Head up . . . you look beautiful. Very slowly turn to me . . .

Anna *takes her shots. They look at each other.*

Good.

Blackout.

Scene Three

Early evening.

Dan *is in his flat sitting at a table with a computer. There is a Newton's Cradle on the table. Writerly sloth, etc.*

Larry *is sitting at his desk with a computer.* **Larry** *is wearing a white coat.*

They are in separate rooms.

The scene is silent. Their 'dialogue' appears on a large screen simultaneous to their typing it.

Dan   Hallo

Larry   hi

Dan   do you come here often?

Larry   ?

Dan   Net

Larry   1st time

Dan   A Virgin. Welcome. What's your name?

Larry   Larry. U?

Beat.

Dan   Anna

Larry   Nice 2 meet U

Pause.

Dan   I love COCK.

Pause.

Larry *(speaking)*   Good evening . . .

Larry *(typing)*   Youre v. forward

Dan   This web site is called LONDON FUCK. Do you want sex?

Larry   yes. describe u

Dan   30s dark hair big mouth epic tits.

Larry   define epic

Dan   36DD

Larry   Nice legs?

Dan   Y.

Larry   Becos i want 2 know

Dan *smiles.*

Dan   No, 'Y' means 'Yes'.

Larry   O

Dan   I want to suck you senseless

Larry   be my guest

Dan   Wear my wet knickers

Larry   ok

Dan   Well hung?

Larry   9£

(*Speaking.*) Shit.

9"

Dan   GET IT OUT

Pause. **Larry** *considers this proposition. The phone on* **Larry**'*s desk rings. Loud. He jumps.*

Larry (*speaking*)   Wait.

Larry (*typing*)   wait

Larry *picks up the phone.* **Dan** *lights a cigarette.*

(*Speaking.*) Hallo? What's the histology? Progressive? No,

sounds like an atrophy. Bye.

He puts the phone down and goes back to his keyboard.

Dan *clicks the balls on his Newton's Cradle.*

Larry   hallo?

Dan *looks at his screen.*

Larry   anna?
(*speaking*)   Bollocks.

(*typing*)   ANNA? WHERE RU?

Dan   Hey, big Larry, what do you wank about?

Larry (*speaking*)   You name it.

Larry (*typing*)   Ex-girlfriends

Dan   Not current g-friends?

Larry   Never.

Dan   Tell me your sex-ex fantasy

Larry   Hotel room ... they tie me up, tease me, won't let me come. They fight over me, 6 tonges on my cock, ballls, perineum etc.

Dan   All hail the Sultan of Twat?

Larry *laughs.*

Larry   Anna, wot do U wank about?

Dan *considers.*

Dan   Strangers.

Larry   details ...

Dan   They form a Q and I attend to them like a cum hungry bitch, 1 in each hole and both hands.

Larry *mentally counts.*

Larry 5?

Dan mmm

Larry's *phone rings. He picks up the receiver and replaces it without answering. Then takes it off the hook.*

Larry then?

Dan They cum in my mouth arse tits cunt hair.

Larry (*speaking*) Jesus.

Larry (*typing*) then?

Dan i lik it off like the the dirty slut I am. Wait, have to type with 1 hand ... I'm cuming right now ... (*He types with one hand.*) ohohohohohohoooooooooj67r86709o78-rt7uy45ws6teh4fnijykolhgugfyyrkjns5r6yuhkjgl, ov6tk8ijmogjulblhufkgmiyg

Pause.

Larry was it good?

Dan I'm quivering.

Larry I'm shocked

Dan PARADISE SHOULD BE SHOCKING

Larry RU4 real?

Dan Y ... Meet me ...

Larry serious?

Dan Y

Larry when

Dan now

Larry can't. I'm a Dr. Hav to do rounds.

Dan *laughs.*

Dan Don't be a pussy. Life without risk is death. Desire, like the world, is an accident. The best sex is anonymous.

We live as we dream, ALONE. I'll make you come like a train.

Larry *flicks through his diary.*

Larry   Tomorrow, 1pm, where?

Dan *thinks.*

Dan   Hackney Marshes.

Larry   Somewhere more central?

Dan   Aquarium, London Zoo.

Larry   1pm

Dan   And then a hotel . . .

Larry   how will i know U?

Dan   bring white coat.

Larry   ?

Dan   Dr + coat = horn 4 me

Larry   ok

Dan   I send you a rose my love . . .

Larry   ?

Dan   (@)

\ |
 |/
 |

Larry   thanks, bye anna

Dan   bye larry xxxxx

Larry   xxxxxxx

They look at their screens.

Blackout.

Scene Four

The Aquarium.

Afternoon.

Larry *is waiting in the darkened room. He holds a single red rose. He looks at the fish. He looks at his watch. He stuffs the rose in his coat pocket. He turns to go.*

Anna *enters. She has a guide book, also her camera.*

Larry *stares at her. Smiles. She vaguely smiles back. She looks at the fish.*

Larry   It beats Hackney Marshes . . .

Anna *nods, acknowledging small talk from a stranger.*

Do you like fish?

Anna   I love them.

Larry *smiles.*

Larry   You're late . . .

Anna *turns.*

Doesn't matter.

She turns back to the fish.

Larry *unbuttons his overcoat and holds it open. He is wearing his white coat underneath.*

I've got the coat . . .

Anna *turns, astonished.*

Anna   Yes, you have . . .

Larry   The white coat . . .

Anna   So I see.

Larry   I'm Larry . . . *(dirty)* 'the doctor'.

Anna   Hallo, Doctor Larry.

Larry   Feel free to call me . . . 'The Sultan'.

She smiles, he smiles back.

Larry   I can't believe these things actually happen.

Beat.

I thought . . . if you turned up . . . that you'd be a dog . . .
but you're bloody gorgeous.

Beat.

You mentioned a hotel . . . no rush. Actually, there is, I've
got to be in surgery by three.

Anna   Are you having an operation?

Larry (*laughs*)   No, I'm doing one.

Anna   On who?

Larry   It's confidential.

Anna   I don't mean to offend but have you got some ID?

Larry   Yes . . .

He hands her his wallet, she looks at a card in it.

Anna   You really are a doctor?

Larry   I said I was.

Sudden panic.

You are Anna?

Anna   Yes. I'm sorry, have we met somewhere?

Larry   Don't play games, you nymph of the Net. Mrs Big
Mouth, Miss Epic Tits. You were fucking filthy *yesterday*.

Anna   Was I?

Larry   'Wear my wet knickers,' 'Suck me senseless,' 'I'm a
cum hungry bitch typing with one . . .'

Pause.

Why do I feel like a pervert?

Anna   I think you're the victim of a medics prank.

Larry *considers.*

Larry   I am *so* sorry.

He begins to exit, stops.

No, we spoke on the Net but . . . now you've seen me . . .
you don't – it's fine. I'm not going to get upset about it.

Anna   Why are you upset then?

Larry   I'm not, I'm frustrated.

Anna   I don't even have a computer, I'm a photographer.

Larry   So why did you let me burble on about sex like a
lunatic?

Anna   Because I thought you were a lunatic.

Larry   No, where were you between the hours of 5.45
and 6.00 p.m. yesterday?

Anna   I was in a café seeing . . . an acquaintance.

Larry   Name?

Anna   Alice Ayres.

Larry   The nature of your business?

Anna   Photographic business. Where were *you* between
those hours?

Larry   On the Net talking to you.

Anna   No.

Larry   Well, I was talking to someone.

Anna   Pretending to be me.

Beat.

(*Smiling.*) You were talking to Daniel Woolf.

Larry   Who?

Anna   He's Alice's boyfriend. She told me yesterday that he plays around on the Net. It's him.

Larry   No, I was talking to a woman.

Anna   How do you know?

Larry   Because ... believe me, she was a woman, I got a huge ... she was a woman.

Anna   No she wasn't.

Larry   She wasn't, was she ...

Anna   No.

Larry   What a CUNT. Sorry.

Anna   I'm a grown-up, cunt away.

Larry   Thanks.

Beat.

This 'bloke' ...

Anna   Daniel Woolf ...

Larry   How do you know him?

Anna   I don't know him really. I took his photo for a book he wrote.

Larry   I hope it sank without trace.

Anna   It's on its way.

Larry (*jubilant*)   There is justice in the world. What's it called?

Anna   'The Aquarium.'

Larry (*furious*)   What a prick. He's advertising.

Beat.

Why? Why would he pretend to be you?

Anna   He likes me.

Larry   Funny way of showing it. Can't he send you flowers?

Larry *disconsolately produces the crumpled rose from his coat pocket. He hands it to* **Anna**.

Anna   Thanks.

Beat.

Larry   Is he in love with you?

Anna   I don't know. No.

Larry   Are you in love with him?

Anna   I hardly know him, no.

Larry   But you're sort of . . . interested?

Anna   I think he's . . . interesting.

Pause.

Wonderful thing the Internet . . .

Larry   Oh yes.

Anna   The possibility of genuine global communication. The last great democratic medium.

Larry   Absolutely, it's the future.

Anna   Two boys tossing in cyberspace.

Larry   *He* was the tosser. I'll say this for him, he can write.

Pause. **Larry** *looks at her, he should go but decides to continue talking to her.*

So what are you doing here?

Anna   Looking at fish.

Larry *considers.*

Larry   Fish; you've got to respect them.

Pause.

Anna   Have you?

Larry   Well, yes. We were fish.

Anna   What?

Larry   Long ago. Before we were apes.

Larry *looks at her, sees she is unhappy.*

Larry   Are you all right?

Anna *nods.*

You can tell me . . .

Anna   Because you're a doctor?

Larry   Because I'm here.

Beat.

Crying is allowed.

Anna   I'm not allowed. Thanks, anyway.

Larry   I'm famed for my bedside manner.

Anna (*raising her camera*)   Say cheese.

Larry (*covering his face*)   Don't, I look like a criminal in photos.

Anna   Please, it's my birthday.

Larry (*dropping his hands*)   Really?

Anna *takes his photo.*

Anna   Yes, really.

Pause. They look at each other.

Larry   Happy birthday.

Blackout.

Scene Five

Gallery.

Evening.

Alice *is looking at a huge photograph of herself. She has a bottle of lager. She wears a black dress.*

Dan *has a glass of wine. A slightly shabby black suit. He looks at* **Alice** *looking at the image.*

Dan   Cheers.

She turns. They drink. **Dan** *looks at the photo.*

Looking good. You're the belle of the bullshit. You look great.

Alice   I'm *here.*

Dan *looks at* **Alice***, smiles.*

Alice   A man came into the café this morning and he said, 'Hey, waitress, what are you waiting for?'

Dan   Funny guy.

Alice   And I said, 'I'm waiting for a man to come in here and fuck me sideways with a beautiful line like that.'

Dan   What did he do?

Alice   He asked for a cup of tea with two sugars.

Pause.

I'm waiting for *you.*

Dan   To do what?

Alice   Leave me.

Dan (*concerned*)   I'm not going to leave you. I totally love you. What is this?

Alice   Please let me come . . .

Dan *turns away.*

Alice   I want to be there for you. Why are you ashamed of me?

Dan   I'm not. I've told you I want to be alone.

Alice   Why?

Dan   To grieve . . . to think.

Alice   I love you, you fucker, why won't you let me?

Dan   It's only a weekend.

Alice   We've never spent a weekend in the country.

Dan   Well . . . we will.

Pause.

Harry's here, pissed as a newt. Wants me to go back to obits. Says they miss me.

Alice   Poor Harry, you know he's in love with you.

Dan   No he's not. Is he?

Alice   Yes. Do you want to go back?

Dan   We're very poor.

Alice   What about your writing?

Dan *shrugs.*

Dan   Look . . . I'm going to say hallo and goodbye to Anna and then I'll get a cab to the station, OK? Buster . . .

Dan *kisses her forehead.*

Alice   Kiss my lips . . .

Dan   Sorry.

He kisses her on the lips.

I'll call you as soon as I get there.

Dan *exits.* **Alice** *sits, lights a cigarette, using her bottle as an ashtray.*

Larry *enters. He is wearing a suit and a black cashmere sweater*

*with a collar. He has a bottle of wine and a glass. He is slightly
drunk.* **Alice** *looks at him, curious.*

Larry   Evening. Fellow refugee escaping from the
glittering babble?

Beat.

Larry *looks at the photo and then at his exhibition price-list.*

No, you are . . . 'Young Woman, London.' Fantastic photo,
do you like it?

Alice   Yes.

Larry   What were you so sad about?

Alice   Life.

Larry   What's that then?

Alice *smiles.*

Larry (*gesturing to the photos*)   What d'you reckon?

Alice   You want to talk about art?

Larry   I know it's vulgar to discuss 'the work' at an
opening of 'the work' but someone's got to do it. Serious,
what d'you think?

Alice   It's a lie. It's a bunch of sad strangers
photographed beautifully. And all the rich fuckers who
appreciate art say it's beautiful because that's what they
want to see. But the people in the photos are sad and
alone but the pictures make the world seem beautiful. So,
the exhibition is reassuring which makes it a lie and
everyone loves a big fat lie.

Larry   I'm the artist's boyfriend.

Alice   Bastard.

Larry   Larry.

Alice   Alice. You're Anna's boyfriend?

Larry   A princess can kiss a toad.

Alice   A frog.

Larry Toad.

Alice Frog.

Larry Fuck it – frog, toad, *otter*. They're all the same.

Alice How long have you been seeing her?

Larry Four months. We're in the first flush, it's paradise, all my nasty habits amuse her. You shouldn't smoke.

Alice Fuck off.

Larry I'm a doctor, I'm supposed to say things like that.

Alice *now realises where she's seen him before.*

Alice Want one?

Larry No. Yes. No, fuck it, yes. No. I've given up.

He watches her smoking.

Pleasure and self-destruction – the perfect poison.

She looks at him, she knows he's flirting with her.

Anna told me your bloke wrote a book. Any good?

Alice Of course.

Larry It's about you, isn't it?

Alice Some of me.

Larry Oh? What did he leave out?

Alice The truth.

Beat.

Larry Is he here? Your bloke.

Alice Yes. He's talking to your bird.

Larry *effects not to care.*

Larry So . . . you were a stripper?

Alice Yes, end of conversation.

Larry *sees the scar on* **Alice***'s leg.*

Larry   Mind if I ask how you got that?

Alice   You've asked me this before.

Larry   When?

Alice   Two . . . no, two and a half years ago. I was in casualty, you looked at my leg.

Larry   How did you remember me?

Alice   It was a memorable day. You didn't really want to stop but you did. You were off for a crafty smoke. You gave me a cigarette.

Larry   Well, I don't smoke now and nor should you.

Alice   So you used to go and smoke . . . on the sly?

Larry   Yeah, in a little park near the hospital.

Alice   Postman's Park?

Larry   That's the one. And . . . the scar?

Alice   A mafia hit-man broke my leg.

Larry   Really?

Alice   Absolutely.

Larry   Doesn't look like a break . . .

Alice   What does it look like?

Larry   Like something went into it. A knife maybe . . .

Alice   When I was eight . . . some metal went into my leg when my parents' car crashed . . . when they died. Happy now?

Larry   Sorry, it was none of my business. I'm supposed to be off-duty.

Alice   Is it nice being good?

Larry (*smiling*)   I'm not good.

He looks at her.

What about you?

She looks away.

I'm seeing my first private patient tomorrow. Tell me I'm not a wanker . . .

Alice   You're not a wanker.

Larry   Thanks. You take care.

Alice   I will, you too.

Alice *exits.* **Larry** *watches her go.* **Larry** *exits as* **Dan** *enters elsewhere.* **Dan** *carries a coat and a small suitcase. He waits, nervously.* **Anna** *enters.*

Pause. They look at each other.

Anna   I can't talk for long.

Dan   Bit of a do, isn't it?

Anna   Yeah, I hate it.

Dan   But you're good at it.

Beat.

So, he's a dermatologist. Can you get more boring than that?

Anna   Obituarist?

Dan   Failed novelist, please.

Anna   I was sorry about your book.

Dan   Thanks, I blame the title.

Anna   You must write another one.

Dan   Why can't failure be attractive?

Anna   It's not a failure.

Dan   It's perceived to be, therefore it is. Pathetically, I needed praise. A *real* writer is . . . above such concerns.

Anna   Romantic tosh.

Dan   Ever had bad reviews? Well, shut up then.

Pause.

Talk to 'Lazza' about photography, do you? Is he a fan of Man Ray or Karsh? He'll bore you.

Anna   No he won't. He doesn't, actually.

Dan (*exasperated*)   I cannot believe I made this happen. What were you doing there?

Beat.

Thinking of me?

Anna   No. How's Alice?

Dan   She's fine. Do you love him?

Anna   Yes.

Dan   You're not going to marry him?

Anna   I don't know.

Dan   Don't. Marry me. Children, everything. You don't want his children . . . three little stooges in white coats. Don't marry him, marry me. Grow old with me . . . die with me . . . wear a battered cardigan on the beach in Bournemouth . . . marry me.

Anna (*laughing*)   I don't know you.

Dan   Yes you do. I couldn't feel what I feel for you unless you felt it too.

Anna   I haven't seen you for a year.

Dan   Yes you have. We've bumped into each other in the street, twice. I manufactured it once, you the other.

Anna   And you just nodded.

Dan   I was scared you didn't feel it too. I felt guilty about Alice. Anna, we're in love, it's not our fault, stop wasting his time.

Anna   I love him. He's a good man. He won't leave me.

Dan   *I* won't leave you. I love your work by the way, it's tragic.

Anna   Thanks.

Dan   I know this isn't . . . appropriate, I'm going to my father's funeral – come with me.

Anna   Stop. Your father died?

Dan   It's fine, I hated him. No, I didn't, I don't care, I care about this. Come with me, spend a weekend with me, then decide.

Anna   What about Alice?

Dan   She'll survive. I can't be her father any more. You want to believe he's . . . 'the one' . . . it's not real, you're scared of this.

Anna   There is no 'this'. I love him, he's kind.

Dan   (*ferocious*)   Don't give me 'kind'. 'Kind' is dull, 'kind' will kill you. Alice is 'kind', even *I'm* 'kind', anyone can be fucking 'kind'. (*Gentle*) I cannot live without you.

Anna   You can, you do.

Dan   This is not me, I don't do this. Don't you see? All the language is old, there are no new words . . . I love you, I 'fucking' love you. I need you. I can't think, I can't work, I can't breathe. We are going to die. Please. Save me. Look at me. Tell me you're not in love with me.

She looks at him.

Anna   I'm not in love with you.

Pause.

Dan   You just lied. See me next week. Please, Anna . . . I'm begging you . . . I'm your stranger . . . jump . . .

Silence. They are close. **Larry** *has entered, he is looking at them.* **Dan** *nods to him.* **Larry** *nods.* **Dan** *goes to exit.*

Anna   Your coat.

Dan *picks up his coat and suitcase and exits.*

Larry   Hallo, stranger.

Anna   Hallo.

Larry   Intense conversation?

Anna   His father's died.

Beat.

Were you spying?

Larry   Lovingly observing. With a telescope. He's taller than his photo.

Anna   The photo's a headshot.

Larry   Yeah I know, but his head implied a short body . . . but in fact his head is . . . deceptive.

Anna   Deceptive?

Larry   Yes, because he's actually got a long body. He's a stringy fucker.

Beat.

I could have him.

Anna   What?

Larry   If it came to it, in a scrap, I could have him.

Anna *smiles.*

Larry   Did you tell him we call him 'Cupid'?

Anna   No, that's *our* joke.

She strokes his sweater.

Larry   I've never worn cashmere before. Thank you. I'm Cinderella at the ball.

Anna (*charmed*)   You're such a pleb.

Pause.

Larry   I had a chat with young Alice.

Anna   Fancy her?

Larry   'Course. Not as much as you.

Anna   Why?

Larry   You're a woman ... she's a girl. She has the moronic beauty of youth but ... she's got ... 'side'.

Anna   She seems very open to me.

Larry   That's how she wants to seem. You forget you're dealing with a clinical observer of the human carnival.

Anna   Am I now?

Larry   Oh yes.

Anna   You seem more like the cat who got the cream. You can stop licking yourself, you know.

Pause.

Larry   That's the nastiest thing you've ever said to me.

Anna   God, I'm sorry. It was a horrible thing to say. I'm sorry, it's just ... my family's here and friends ... I have no excuse.

Beat.

Larry   Forget it. I know what you mean. I'll stop pawing you.

Beat.

I met your dad.

Anna   I know. He actually said, 'I like him.' He's never said that before ... about anyone. They all adored you. My stepmother thinks you're gorgeous. 'Lovely hands' she said, 'you can imagine him doing his stitching, very sensitively.'

Larry   So ... they didn't think I was ... an oik?

Anna   No. You're not ... you're you and you're wonderful.

Larry   Did you like my folks? They loved you.

Anna   Your mother's got such a . . . kind face.

They look at each other.

Blackout.

Scene Six

Domestic interiors.

Midnight.

Anna *sitting on a chaise-longue.*

Alice *sitting on a small sofa. She is wearing striped pyjamas. She has a side plate with apple segments on it. She is dipping the apple in a jar of honey and eating, slowly.*

They are in separate rooms.

Dan *enters. He carries the brown briefcase seen in Scene One.*

Alice   Where've you been? I was worried.

Beat.

What?

Dan   Work. Had a drink with Harry. You never have one drink with Harry.

Alice   Did you eat? I made some sandwiches, no crusts.

Dan   I'm not hungry.

Pause.

Alice   What?

Dan   This will hurt. I've been with Anna.

Pause.

I'm in love with her. I've been seeing her for a year.

Alice *exits covering her mouth.*

On the other side of the stage: enter **Larry**. **Larry** *has a suitcase, bags, duty-free carrier.*

Larry Don't move. I want to remember this moment for ever; the first time I walked through the door, returning from a business trip, to be greeted by my wife. I have, in this moment, become an adult.

He kisses **Anna**.

Thanks for waiting up, you darling. You goddess. I missed you. Jesus, I'm knackered.

Anna Didn't you sleep on the plane?

Larry Nahh. Because the permed German sleeping next to me was snoring like a *Messerschmitt*. What's the time?

Anna Midnight.

Larry Seven. Time . . . what a tricky little fucker. My head's in two places. My brain actually hurts.

Anna Do you want some food?

Larry Nahh, I ate my 'Scooby Snacks' on the plane. I need a bath.

Anna Shall I run you one?

Larry I'll have a shower. You OK?

Anna Mmhmm.

Larry Sorry I didn't phone. I mean, I did phone but you were out.

Anna How was the hotel?

Larry *takes a bottle of Scotch from his bag of duty-free and swigs it.*

Larry Someone told me . . . that the beautiful people of 'The Paramount Hotel', the concierge and the bell-boys and girls . . . did you know this . . . they're all whores.

Anna Everyone knows that.

Larry I didn't. Want some?

Anna *shakes her head.*

I love New York. What a town: a twenty-four-hour pageant called 'Shit your mind out'. They celebrate the sell-out. It's a Mardi Gras of degradation. Then . . . you arrive back at Heathrow, the first thing you see is this carpet . . . this unbelievable carpet . . . what the fuck colour is the carpet at Heathrow Airport? They must've layed it to reassure foreigners we're not a serious country. God, I stink.

Anna   Are you all right?

Larry   I don't suppose you fancy a friendly poke?

Anna   I've just had a bath.

Larry   I'll see to myself then, in the *Elle Decoration* bathroom.

Anna   You chose that bathroom.

Larry   Yeah and every time I wash in it I feel dirty. It's cleaner than I am. It's got 'attitude'. The mirror says, 'Who the fuck are you?'

Anna   You chose it.

Larry   Doesn't mean I like it. We shouldn't have . . . this.

He gestures vaguely about the room.

Anna   Are you experiencing bourgeois guilt?

Larry   Working-class guilt.

Pause.

Why are you dressed? If you've just had a bath.

Anna   We needed some milk.

Beat.

Larry   Right. You OK?

Anna   Uhhuh. You?

Larry   Yeah.

Larry *exits.* **Alice** *enters. She is wearing the same black coat from Scene One. Also her rucksack from the same scene.*

Alice   I'm going.

Dan   I'm sorry.

Alice   Irrelevant. What are you sorry for?

Dan   For leaving you.

Beat.

Alice   Why didn't you tell me before?

Beat.

Dan   Cowardice.

Alice   Is it because she's clever?

Dan   No, it's because . . . she doesn't need me.

Alice   Do you bring her here?

Dan   Yes.

Alice   She sits here?

Dan   Yes.

Alice   Didn't she get married?

Dan   She stopped seeing me.

Alice   Is that when we went to the country? To celebrate our third anniversary?

Dan   Yes.

Alice   At least have the guts to look at me, you cunt.

Dan *looks at her.*

Alice   Did you phone her? To beg her to come back?

Dan *nods.*

Alice   When you went for your long lonely walks?

Dan   Yes.

Alice   You're a piece of shit.

Dan   Deception is brutal, I'm not pretending otherwise.

Alice   How ... how does it work ... how can you do this to someone?

Dan   I don't know.

Alice   Not good enough. I'm going.

Dan   It's late, it's not safe out there.

Alice   And it's safe in here?

Dan   What about your things?

Alice   I don't need 'things'.

Larry *enters having had his shower, he is wearing a dressing-gown. He hands* **Anna** *a shoe box.*

Larry   The Sultan has returned bearing gifts.

Anna *opens the box and takes out the shoes.*

Dan   Where will you go?

Alice   I'll disappear.

Anna   They're beautiful. Thank you.

Larry   You could wear them to the do on Friday.

Anna *grimaces.*

I've got to put in an appearance, I'm never there. I've got more private patients than BUPA.

Dan *moves to* **Alice**.

Alice   DON'T COME NEAR ME. DON'T FUCKING COME NEAR ME.

Larry   Hey, guess what. Alice was at the Paramount Hotel.

Anna   What?

Larry   They sell arty postcards in the lobby. I bought one to boost your sales.

He finds it in his bag and reads the back.

'Young Woman, London.'

He hands it to her.

And ... I checked for your book in the Museum of
Modern Art – it's there. Someone bloody bought one; this
'artsy' student in ridiculous spectacles. He was drooling over
your photo on the inside cover – fancied you, the little
geek. I was so proud of you, you've broken New York.

Anna   You're wonderful.

Larry   Don't ever forget it.

Larry *exits.*

Alice   Change your mind. Please change your mind.

Pause.

Can I still see you?

Beat.

Dan, can I still see you? Answer me, you fucker.

Dan   I can't see you. If I see you I'll never leave you.

Alice   What will you do if I find someone else?

Dan   Be jealous.

Beat.

Alice   Do you still fancy me?

Dan   Of course.

Pause. She shakes her head.

Alice   You're lying. I've been 'you'.

Beat.

Hold me?

Dan *holds her.*

Alice You did love me?

Dan I'll always love you. You changed my life. I hate hurting you.

Alice So why are you?

Dan Because ... I think I'll be happier with her.

Alice You won't. You'll miss me. No one will ever love you as much as I do.

Dan I know.

Alice Why isn't love enough?

Pause.

I'm the one who leaves. I'm supposed to leave you. I'm the one who leaves.

Beat.

Make some tea ... Buster.

Dan *exits.* **Anna** *and* **Alice** *are alone.* **Larry** *enters. He is wearing trousers and the black cashmere seen in Scene Five.*

Anna Why are you dressed?

Larry Because I think you might be about to leave me and I didn't want to be wearing a dressing-gown.

Pause.

I fucked someone in New York. A whore. I'm sorry.

Beat.

Please don't leave me.

Anna Why?

Larry For sex. I wanted sex. I wore a condom.

Anna Was it ... good?

Larry *huffs and puffs.*

Larry Yes.

Anna Paramount whore?

Larry No . . . Forty . . . something street.

Anna Where did you go?

Larry Her place.

Anna Nice?

Larry Not as nice as ours. I'm really sorry.

Anna Why did you tell me?

Larry I couldn't lie to you.

Anna Why not?

Larry Because I love you.

Beat.

Anna It's fine.

Larry Really? Why?

Anna Because . . .

Anna *looks at her shoes.*

Guilt present?

Larry Love present. Something's wrong . . .

Anna Yes.

Pause.

Larry Are you leaving me?

She nods.

Why?

Anna Dan.

Beat.

Larry Cupid? He's our joke.

Anna I love him.

Pause.

Larry   You're seeing him now . . .

Anna   Yes.

Larry   Since when?

Anna   My opening, last year. I'm disgusting.

Larry   You're phenomenal . . . you're so . . . clever.

Beat.

Why did you marry me?

Anna   I stopped seeing him. I wanted us to work.

Larry   Why did you tell me you wanted children?

Anna   Because I did.

Larry   And now you want children with him?

Anna   Yes. I don't know. I'm sorry.

Beat.

Larry   Why?

Anna   I need him.

Larry   What does that mean?

Anna   He understands me.

Larry   You're mad. We're happy. Aren't we?

Anna   Yes.

Beat.

Larry   Are you going to live with him?

Anna   Yes. You stay here, if you want to.

Larry   I don't give a fuck about . . . 'the spoils'.

Alice *gets up and exits.*

You did this the day we met; let me fucking hang myself, make me feel . . . humiliated, for your amusement. Why didn't you tell me the second I walked in the door?

Anna   I was scared.

Larry   Because you're a coward. You spoilt bitch.

Dan *enters with two cups of tea, he sees* **Alice** *has gone. He exits after her.*

Larry   Are you dressed because you thought I might hit you? What do you think I am?

Anna   I've been hit before.

Larry   Not by me.

Pause.

Is he a good fuck?

Anna   Don't do this.

Larry   Just answer the question. Is he good?

Anna   Yes.

Larry   Better than me?

Anna   Different.

Larry   Better?

Anna   Gentler.

Larry   What does that mean?

Anna   You know what it means.

Larry   Tell me.

Anna   No.

Larry   I treat you like a whore?

Anna   Sometimes.

Larry   Why would that be?

Silence.

Anna   I'm sorry. It's done. You're too –

Larry Don't say it, don't fucking say 'You're too good for me.' I am but don't fucking say it. (*Gently*.) You're making the mistake of your life. You're leaving me because you think you don't deserve happiness. But you do, Anna, you fucking do.

Beat.

Did you have a bath because you had sex with him?

Anna Yes.

Larry So you didn't smell of him? So you'd feel less guilty.

Anna Yes.

Larry And how do you feel?

Anna Guilty.

Larry Do you love me?

Anna Yes.

Larry Big fucking deal.

Pause.

Larry Anna . . . please don't leave me.

She holds him. On the other side of the stage **Dan** *enters, sits.*

Larry Did you do it here?

Anna No.

Larry Why not?

Anna Do you wish we did?

Larry (*hard*) Just tell me the truth.

Anna Yes, we did it here.

Larry Where?

Anna Everywhere.

Larry Here? In here?

Anna Yes.

Larry Where? ·

Anna   Here.

Larry   On this?

Anna   Yes.

Larry   We had our first fuck on this.

Beat.

Think of me?

Beat.

When? When did you do it here? ANSWER THE
FUCKING QUESTION.

Anna (*scared*)   This evening.

Pause.

Larry   Did you come?

Anna   Why are you doing this?

Larry   Because I want to know.

Anna   Yes, I came.

Larry   How many times?

Anna   Twice.

Larry   How?

Anna   First he went down on me and then we fucked.

Larry   Who was where?

Anna (*tough*)   I was on top and then he fucked me from
behind.

Larry   And that's when you came the second time?

Anna   Yes. Why is the sex so important?

Larry   BECAUSE I'M A FUCKING CAVEMAN. Did
you touch yourself while he fucked you?

Anna   Yes.

Larry   You wank for him?

Anna   Sometimes.

Larry   And he does?

Anna   We do everything that people who have sex do.

Larry   You enjoy sucking him off?

Anna   Yes.

Larry   You like his cock?

Anna   I love it.

Larry   You like him coming in your face?

Anna   Yes.

Larry   What does it taste like?

Anna   IT TASTES LIKE YOU BUT SWEETER.

Larry   THAT'S THE SPIRIT. THANK YOU. THANK YOU FOR YOUR HONESTY. NOW FUCK OFF AND DIE, YOU FUCKED-UP SLAG.

Blackout.

Act Two

Scene Seven

Lapdance Club.

Late night.

Larry *is sitting. He is wearing a suit. He had a big, fat line of cocaine fifteen minutes ago.*

Alice *is standing. She is wearing a dress and high heels. She is wearing a wig. She has a garter round her thigh, there is cash in the garter.*

They are in a private room. Music in the distance.

Larry *looks at her. She smiles. She is nice to him.*

Larry   I love you.

Pause.

Alice   Thank you.

Larry   What's this room called?

Alice   The Paradise Suite.

Larry   How many Paradise Suites are there?

Alice   Six.

Larry   Do I have to pay you to talk to me?

Alice   No, but if you want to tip me it's your choice.

He takes out a twenty and puts it in her garter.

Thank you.

Larry   I went to a place like this in New York. This is swish. Pornography has gone up-market – Bully for England. I used to come here twenty years ago . . . it was a punk club . . . the stage was . . . everything is a version of something else.

He takes a slug of his drink.

Twenty years ago, how old were you?

Alice Four.

Larry Christ, when I was in flares you were in nappies.

Alice My nappies were flared.

Larry *laughs.*

Larry Did you see that 'piece' in *The Sunday* ... *Bollock* –
some supplement whore gassing on about Lapdancing –
'The new rock and roll.' What a silly bitch. This is honest
progress, don't you think?

Alice England always imports the best of America.

Larry You have the face of an angel.

Alice Thank you.

Larry What does your cunt taste like?

Alice Heaven.

Larry How long you been doing this?

Alice Three months.

Larry Straight after he left you?

Alice No one left me.

Beat.

Larry Does it turn you on?

Alice Sometimes.

Larry Liar. You're telling me it turns you on because
you think that's what I want to hear. You think I'm turned
on by it turning you on.

Alice The thought of me creaming myself when I strip
for strangers doesn't turn you on?

Larry Put like that ... yes.

She sits with him, close.

Larry   Are you flirting with me?

Alice   Maybe.

Larry   Are you allowed to flirt with me?

Alice   Sure.

Larry   Really?

Alice   No, I'm not, I'm breaking all the rules.

Larry   You're mocking me.

She sits opposite him.

Alice   Yes, I'm allowed to flirt.

Larry   To prise my money from me.

Alice   To prise your money from you I can say or do as I please.

Larry   Except touch.

Alice   We are not allowed to touch.

Larry   Is that a good rule, do you think?

Alice   Oh yes.

Beat.

Larry   Open your legs. Wider.

Larry *looks between her legs.*

What would happen if I touched you now?

Alice   I would call security.

Larry   And what would they do?

Alice   They would ask you to leave and ask you not to come back.

Larry   And if I refused to leave?

Alice   They would remove you. This is a two-way mirror.

She nods to the audience.

There are cameras in the ceiling.

Beat. **Larry** *glances up and to the audience.*

Larry   I think it's best that I don't attempt to touch you.

Beat.

I'd like to touch you . . . later.

Alice   I'm not a whore.

Larry   I wouldn't pay.

Beat.

Why the fuck did he leave you?

Alice   What's your job?

Larry   A question. You've asked me a question.

Alice   So?

Larry   It's a chink in your armour.

Alice   I'm not wearing armour.

Larry   Yes you are. I'm in the skin trade.

Alice   You own strip clubs?

Larry   Do I look like the sort of man who owns strip clubs?

Alice   Yes.

He looks in the mirror.

Larry   Define that look.

Alice   Rich.

Larry   Close your legs. I don't own strip clubs.

Alice   Do you own golf clubs?

Larry   You know what I do. Why are you calling yourself Jane?

Alice   Because it's my name.

Larry   But we both know it isn't. You're all protecting your identities. The girl in there who calls herself Venus. What's her real name?

Alice   Pluto.

Larry   You're cheeky.

Alice   Would you like me to stop being cheeky?

Larry   No.

Beat.

Alice   What's *your* name?

Larry   Daniel.

Alice   Daniel the Dermatologist.

Larry   I never told you my job.

Alice   I guessed.

Beat.

Larry   You're strong. There's another one in there (judging by the scars, a recent patient of Doctor Tit) she calls herself 'Cupid'. Who's going to tell her Cupid was a bloke?

Alice   He wasn't a bloke. He was a little boy.

Pause.

Larry   I'd like you to tell me your name. Please.

He gives her £20.

Alice   Thank you. My name is Jane.

Larry   Your real name.

He gives her £20.

Alice   Thank you. My real name is Jane.

Larry   Careful.

He gives her £20.

Alice   Thank you. It's still Jane.

Larry   Your name . . .

He gives her £20.

Alice   Thank you. Jane.

Pause.

Larry   I've got another five hundred quid here.

He takes out the money.

Why don't I give you all this money and you tell me what your real name is. Alice.

He offers her the money. She tries to take it. He won't let go.

Alice   I promise . . .

He gives her the money.

Alice   My real name is plain . . . Jane . . . Jones.

Larry   I may be rich but I'm not stupid.

Alice   What a shame, Doc, I love 'em rich and stupid.

Larry   DON'T FUCK AROUND WITH ME.

Alice   I apologise.

Larry   Accepted. All the girls in this hell-hole; the pneumatic robots, the coked-up baby dolls – and you're no different, you all use stage names to con yourselves you're someone else so you don't feel ashamed when you show your cunts and arseholes to complete fucking strangers. I'm trying to have a conversation here.

Alice   You're out of cash, Buster.

Larry   I've paid for the room.

Alice   This is extra.

Larry   We met last year.

Alice Wrong girl.

Larry I know you're in grief. I know you're . . . destroyed. Talk to me.

Alice I am.

Larry Talk to me in real life.

Silence.

I didn't know you'd be here. I know who you are. I love your scar, I love everything about you that hurts.

Larry *breaks down.*

I miss her. I love her. She won't even see me. TALK TO ME.

Larry *sobs.*

You feel the same, I know you feel the same.

Alice You can't cry here.

Larry Hold me, let me hold you.

Alice We are not allowed to touch.

Pause.

Larry Come home with me, Alice. It's safe. Let me look after you.

Alice I don't need looking after.

Larry Everyone needs looking after.

Alice I'm not your revenge fuck.

Beat.

Larry I'll pay you.

Alice I don't need your money.

Larry You *have* my money.

Alice Thank you.

Larry Thank you, thank you. Is that some kind of rule?

Alice   I'm just being polite.

Beat.

Larry   Get a lot of men in here, crying their guts out?

Alice   Occupational hazard.

Beat.

Larry   Have you ever desired a customer?

Alice   Yes.

Larry   Put me out of my misery, do you . . . desire me? Because I'm being pretty fucking honest about my feelings for you.

Alice   Your feelings?

Larry   Whatever.

Alice   No. I don't desire you.

Silence.

Larry   Thank you. Thank you sincerely for your honesty. Next question; do you think it's possible you could perceive me as something other than a sad fruit machine spewing out money?

Alice   That's the transaction; you're the customer, I'm the service.

Larry   Hey, we're in a strip club let's not debate sexual politics.

Alice   Debate?

Larry   You're asking for a smack, gorgeous.

Alice   No I'm not.

Pause.

Larry   But you are gorgeous.

Alice   Thank you.

Beat.

Larry Will you lend me my cab fare?

Alice (*laughing*) No.

Larry I'll give it back to you tomorrow.

Alice Company policy, you give us the money.

Larry And what do we get in return?

Alice We're nice to you.

Larry And we get to see you naked.

Alice It's beautiful.

Larry Except . . . you think you haven't given us anything of yourselves. You think because you don't love us or desire us or even like us you think you've won.

Alice It's not a war.

Larry *laughs.*

Larry But you do give us something of yourselves: you give us imagery . . . and we do with it what we will.

Pause.

You don't understand the territory. Because you *are* the territory.

Beat.

I could ask you to strip right now.

Alice Yes.

Larry Would you?

Alice Sure. Do you want me to?

Larry No. Alice . . . tell me something true.

Alice Lying is the most fun a girl can have without taking her clothes off. But it's better if you do.

Larry You're cold. You're all cold at heart.

Larry *stares into the two-way mirror.*

WHAT DO YOU HAVE TO DO TO GET A BIT OF
INTIMACY ROUND HERE?

Alice Well, maybe next time I'll have worked on my
intimacy.

Larry No, I'll tell you what's going to *work*. What's going
to *work* is that you're going to take your clothes off right
now and you're going to turn round very slowly and bend
over and touch the fucking floor for my viewing pleasure.

Alice That's what you want?

Larry What else could I want?

She looks straight at him and begins to undress, slowly.

Blackout.

Scene Eight

Concert hall.

Evening.

Dan *is sitting at a small table with a drink. Smoking. He flicks
through a programme. He waits. Music in the distance.*

Anna *arrives. He stands, kisses her.*

Anna Sorry. I'm really sorry.

Dan What happened?

Anna Traffic. Why didn't you go in?

Dan You've got the tickets.

Applause from the concert hall.

Anna Shall we go in now?

Dan I'm not in the mood for Wagner. Have a drink.

He gestures to the table, **Anna***'s drink is waiting for her. She sits.*

Anna Thanks.

She drinks.

Dan   So ... How was it?

Anna   We met ...

Dan   Where?

Anna   A café near his work.

Dan   And?

Anna   Then we left.

Dan   And?

Anna   There is no 'and'.

Dan   You haven't seen him for four months, there must be an 'and'.

She shrugs.

What did you talk about?

Anna   Him, us, you know.

Dan   How is he?

Anna   Terrible.

Dan   How's his work?

Anna   He's gone 'private'.

Dan   How does he square that with his politics?

Anna   He's not much concerned with politics at present.

Dan   So he misses you?

Anna   Yes.

Dan   Was he weeping all over the place?

Anna   Some of the time.

Dan   Poor bastard. Was he ... difficult?

Beat.

Anna   Are you angry I saw him?

Dan   No. I just don't understand why you did. I haven't seen Alice.

Anna   You can't see Alice, you don't know where she is.

Dan   I haven't tried to find her.

Anna   He's been begging me to see him for months. You know why I saw him. I saw him so he'd ... sign.

Dan   You could've sent them to him.

Anna   I did, he sent them back.

Dan   So has he signed?

Anna   Yes.

Dan   Congratulations. You are now a divorcee – double divorcee. Sorry. How do you feel?

Anna   Tired.

Beat.

Dan   Shall we go and eat?

Anna   I'm not hungry.

Silence. **Dan** *looks at her.*

Dan   You fucked him, didn't you?

Pause.

Anna   Yes. This afternoon. I'm sorry.

Dan   What do you expect me to do?

Anna   Understand ... ?

Beat.

Dan   Why didn't you lie to me?

Anna   I never want to lie to you.

Dan   (*light*)   What's so great about the truth? Try lying for a change, it's the currency of the world.

Anna   We said we'd always tell each other the truth.

Beat.

I did it so he'd leave us alone. I did what he wanted and now he will go away. I didn't *give* him anything.

Dan   Your body?

Anna   Before you there were other people. Trawl the convents, Dan, find yourself a virgin.

Dan   It's different.

Dan *reaches for his cigarettes.*

Anna   If Alice came to you . . . desperate, in tears, with all that love still between you; and she said she needed you to want her so that she could get over you, you would do it. I wouldn't like it either but I would forgive you because it's . . . a mercy fuck . . . a sympathy fuck. Moral rape, everyone does it. It's kindness.

Dan   No, it's cowardice. You don't have the guts to let him hate you.

Beat.

Did you enjoy it?

Anna   No.

Dan   So you hated every second of it?

Beat.

Did you come?

Anna   No.

Dan   Did you fake it?

Anna   Yes.

Dan   Why?

Anna   To make him think I enjoyed it, why do you think?

Dan   If you were just his slag, why did you give him the pleasure of thinking you'd enjoyed it?

Anna I don't know, I just did.

Dan You fake it with me?

Anna Yes, yes I do. I fake one in three, all right?

Dan Really?

Anna I haven't counted.

Dan (*hard*) Tell me the truth.

Anna Occasionally . . . I have faked it. It's not important.
You don't *make* me come. I come, you're . . . in the area
. . . providing . . . valiant assistance.

Dan You make *me* come.

Anna You're a man, you'd come if the tooth fairy winked
at you.

Dan *smiles.*

Dan You're late because you've come straight here from
being with him.

Pause.

Anna Yes.

Dan Long session.

She tries to touch him, he pulls away.

Anna Dan be bigger than . . . jealous. Please be bigger.

Dan What could be bigger than jealousy? You sit here
stinking of spunk and tell me to be bigger. Cheers.

He stands. Drinks.

Pause.

Anna Why won't you kiss me when we're fucking? You
don't even like it when I say I love you.

Beat.

I'm on your side. Talk to me.

Dan   It hurts. I'm ashamed. I know it's illogical and I do understand but I hate you.

Beat.

I love you and I don't like other men fucking you. Is that so weird?

Anna   No. Yes. It was only sex.

Dan   If you can still fuck him you haven't left him.

Pause.

It's gone . . . we're not innocent any more.

Anna   Don't stop loving me. I can see it draining out of you.

Beat.

I'm sorry, it was a stupid thing to do. It meant nothing. If you love me enough you'll forgive me.

Dan   Are you testing me?

Anna   No. I do understand.

Dan   No. *He* understands.

He looks at her.

All I can see is *him* all over you.

Beat.

He's clever, your *ex*-husband – I almost admire him.

Silence.

Anna   Where are you? Alice?

Dan (*smiles*)   I was reading the paper once. She wanted some attention. She crouched down on the carpet and pissed right in front of me. Isn't that the most charming thing you've ever heard?

Anna   I was charmed by the battered cardigan on the

beach. Why did you swear eternal love when all you wanted was a fuck?

Dan I didn't just want a fuck, I wanted you.

Anna You wanted excitement. Love bores you.

Dan No, it disappoints me.

Beat.

I think you enjoyed it. He wheedles you into bed ... the old jokes, the strange familiarity ... where was it?

Anna His new surgery.

Dan Nice?

Anna OK.

Dan I think you had a whale of a time. And the truth is ... I'll never know unless I ask *him*.

Anna Well, why don't you?

Distant applause from the concert hall.

I did it because I feel guilty and because I pity him. You know that, don't you?

Dan Yes.

Anna I didn't do it to hurt you. It's not all about you.

Dan I know. Let's go home.

Blackout.

Scene Nine

Museum.

Afternoon.

A glass cabinet containing a life-size model of a Victorian child. A girl, dressed in rags. Behind her a model of a London street circa 1880s.

Alice *is alone. She is wearing a cashmere sweater. She is looking at the exhibit. She is holding a small package.*

Larry *enters. He watches her.*

Larry   Hallo, gorgeous.

Alice *turns.*

Alice   You're late, you old fart.

Larry   Sorry.

They kiss, warmly.

You minx.

Alice   Why?

Larry *tugs the sweater.*

Alice   The sacred sweater. I'll give it back.

Larry   It suits you. Keep it.

Alice *hands him the package.*

Alice   Happy birthday.

Larry   Thank you.

Beat.

I'm late because I walked through Postman's Park to get here. And I had a little look at the memorial . . .

Alice   Oh.

Larry   Yeah . . . oh.

Pause. **Larry** *looks at the exhibit. Smiles at* **Alice**.

Alice   Do you hate me?

Larry   No, I adore you.

Alice   Do we have to talk about it?

Larry   Not if you don't want to.

She kisses him.

Alice   Thank you. I've got a surprise for you.

Larry   You're full of them.

Alice *looks at* **Larry***'s watch.*

Alice   Wait here.

Alice *exits.* **Larry** *sits. He opens his package. Looks inside, smiles.*

Anna *enters looking at her watch. She has a guide book and her camera. She is wearing the shoes* **Larry** *gave her in Scene Six. She sees* **Larry***. Stops.* **Larry** *looks up, sees her. Pause.*

Anna   What are *you* doing here?

Larry   I'm . . . lazing on a Sunday afternoon. You?

Anna   I'm meeting Alice.

Larry   Alice?

Anna   Dan's Alice, ex-Alice. She phoned me at the studio this morning . . . she wants her negatives . . .

Larry   Right . . .

Beat.

Anna   You don't go to museums.

Larry   The evidence would suggest otherwise.

Beat.

Anna   Are you OK?

Larry   Yeah, you?

Anna   Fine. It's your birthday today.

Larry   I know.

Anna   I thought of you this morning.

Larry   Lucky me.

Anna   Happy birthday.

Larry   Thank you.

Beat.

Anna   Present?

Larry   Yeah.

Anna   What is it?

Larry   A Newton's Cradle.

Anna   Who from?

Larry   My dad.

Anna   Joe?

Silence.

Larry   It's from Alice. I'm fucking her ... that's why I'm here. I'm fucking Alice. She's set us up. I had no idea you were meeting her.

Pause.

Anna   You're old enough to be her ancestor.

Larry   Yup, disgusting, isn't it.

Anna   You should be ashamed.

Larry (*smiling*)   I am.

Anna   How ... ?

Larry (*vague*)   I went to a club, she happened to be there.

Anna   A club?

Larry   Yeah, a club.

Anna   You don't go to clubs.

Larry   I'm reliving my youth.

Anna   Was it a strip club?

Larry   You know, I can't remember.

Beat.

Jealous? Ah well . . .

Anna   When did it start?

Larry   About a month ago.

Anna   Before or after I came to your surgery?

Larry   The night before. She made me strip for her.

Anna   I don't want to know.

Larry   I know.

Beat.

Did you tell your 'soul-mate' about *that* afternoon?

Anna   Of course.

Larry   How did he take it?

She considers.

Anna   Like a man.

She looks at him.

Larry   I told you it was best to be truthful.

Anna   You're sly.

Larry   Am I?

Beat.

You love your guide books. You look like a tourist.

Anna   I feel like one. Please don't hate me.

Larry   It's easier than loving you.

Pause.

Me and Alice . . . it's nothing.

Anna   Nice nothing?

Larry   Very.

They look at each other.

Since we're talking, could you have a word with your
solicitor? I'm still awaiting confirmation of our divorce.

Alice *enters.*

Alice Ahh, the happy couple.

Larry I think I'll leave you to it.

Alice Good idea, we don't want *him* here while we're working, do we?

Larry (*to* **Anna**) Bye.

He kisses **Alice**.

(*To* **Alice**.) Later, Minx. (*To* **Anna**.) Nice shoes by the way.

Larry *exits.*

Anna How did you get so brutal?

Alice I lived a little.

Alice *strokes the sweater.*

Anna You're primitive.

Alice Yeah, I am. How's Dan?

Anna Fine.

Alice How's his work?

Anna He's been made editor.

Alice Of obituaries?

Anna Yes.

Alice How come?

Anna The previous editor died.

Alice Harry Masters?

Anna *softens, slightly, realising* **Alice** *knew him.*

Anna Yes. Alcohol poisoning. Dan was very upset, he sat with him for a week while he died.

Alice Did you tell him you were seeing me?

Anna No.

Alice Do you cut off his crusts?

Anna   Sorry?

Alice   Do you cut off his crusts?

Anna   What do you want?

Alice   I want my negatives.

Anna *gives her a large brown envelope.*

Alice   What's your latest project, Anna?

Anna   Derelict buildings.

Alice   How nice, the beauty of ugliness.

Anna   What are you doing with Larry?

Alice   Showing him a good time. I like your bed by the way. I'm stripping again.

Anna   I know.

Alice   You should come to the club sometime, show everyone what you've got. Larry used to wander around like a zombie, blubbing into his ashtray. We called him 'Happy Larry'. I wish you could've seen it. It might've helped you develop a conscience.

Anna   I know what I've done.

Alice   His big thing at the moment is how upset his family are. Apparently, they all worship you, they can't understand why you had to ruin everything. He spends hours staring up my arsehole like there's going to be some answer there. Any ideas, Anna? Why don't you go back to him and we can all be happy again.

Anna   And then would Dan go back to you?

Alice   Maybe.

Anna   Ask him.

Alice   I'm not a beggar.

Anna   Dan left you, I didn't force him to go.

Alice   You made yourself available, don't weasel out of it.

Anna Fucking Larry was a big mistake.

Alice Yeah, well, everyone fucks Larry round here.

Anna You're Dan's little girl, he won't like it.

Alice So don't tell him, I think you owe me that.

Anna *looks away.*

Alice You even look beautiful when you cry. The perfect woman.

Anna JUST FUCKING STOP IT.

Alice Now we're talking.

Anna Why now, why come for me now?

Alice Because I felt strong enough. It's taken me five months to convince myself you're not better than me.

Anna It's not a competition.

Alice Yes it is.

Anna I don't want a fight.

Alice So give in.

Beat.

Why did you do this?

Anna (*tough*) I fell in love with him, Alice.

Alice (*laughing*) That's the most stupid expression in the world. 'I fell in love.' As if you had no choice. There's a moment, there's always a moment; I can do this, I can give in to this or I can resist it. I don't know when your moment was but I bet there was one.

Anna Yes, there was.

Alice You didn't fall in love, you gave in to temptation. Don't lie to me.

Anna You fell in love with him too.

Alice No, I chose him. I looked in his briefcase and I

found this ... sandwich ... and I thought, I will give all my love to this stupid, boring, charming man who cuts off his crusts. I didn't *fall* in love, I chose to.

Pause.

Anna You still want him, after everything he's done to you?

Anna You wouldn't understand, he ... buries me.

Anna Hallo?

Alice He makes me invisible.

Anna What are you hiding from?

Alice Everything. Everything's a lie, nothing matters.

Anna Bollocks. Too easy, Alice, it's the cop-out of the age.

Alice Yeah, well, you're old.

Pause.

Anna I am sorry. I had a choice and I chose to be selfish. I'm sorry.

Alice Everyone's selfish. I stole Dan from ... what was her name?

Anna *thinks.*

Anna Ruth.

Alice She went to pieces when he left her.

Anna Did she ever come and see you?

Alice No, she was a faxer not a fighter.

Pause.

Anna Larry told me what you said about my exhibition.

Alice At least your pictures are better than Dan's crappy novel. What a pile of cock. Even the title's shit.

Anna You think so?

Alice   Why didn't he write about something that hurt him? He's such a wimp, he won't go near himself.

Anna   It's easy to say that. I'm not being patronising but you're a child.

Alice   You are being patronising.

Anna   And you are a child. You can't even hear your clock ticking.

Beat.

Alice   So, what are you going to do?

Anna   Think.

Pause.

Is Larry nice to you, in bed?

Alice   OK, Dan's better.

Anna   Rubbish, at least Larry's there.

Alice   Dan's there, in his own quiet way.

Anna   They spend a lifetime fucking and never know how to make love.

Alice   So eat pussy, Anna.

Anna (*weary*)   Oh, I have.

Beat.

Alice   I've got a scar on my leg, Larry's mad about it. He licks it like a dog. Any ideas?

Anna   Dermatology? God knows. This is what we're dealing with; we arrive with our baggage and for a while they're brilliant, they're baggage handlers. We say 'Where's your baggage?' They deny all knowledge of it, they're in love, they have none. Then, just as you're relaxing, a great big juggernaut arrives ... with their baggage. It got held up. The greatest myth men have about women is that we overpack.

Beat.

They love the way we make them feel but not 'us'. They love dreams.

Alice   So do we. You should lower your expectations.

Anna   Who's 'Buster'?

Alice   'Buster'? No idea.

Anna   He says it in his sleep.

Alice *smiles.*

Alice   I've got to go.

Anna   Don't forget your negatives.

Alice   Oh yeah. Thanks.

She hands the envelope to **Anna**.

Must dash. Do the right thing, Anna.

Alice *exits.* **Anna** *looks at the envelope.*

Blackout.

Scene Ten

Larry's *surgery.*

Late afternoon.

On **Larry**'s *desk: laptop computer, phone, a Newton's Cradle. Also in the room, a surgery bed.* **Larry** *seated at his desk.* **Dan** *standing, distraught.*

Silence.

Larry   So . . .

Dan   I want Anna back.

Larry   She's made her choice.

Beat.

Dan   I owe you an apology. I fell in love with her. My intention was not to make you suffer.

Larry *(friendly)*   Where's the apology, you cunt.

Dan   I apologise.

Pause.

If you love her, you'll let her go so she can be . . . happy.

Larry   She doesn't want to be 'happy'.

Dan   Everyone wants to be happy.

Larry   Depressives don't. They want to be unhappy to confirm they're depressed. If they were happy they couldn't be depressed any more, they'd have to go out into the world and live, which can be . . . depressing.

Dan   Anna's not a depressive.

Larry   Isn't she?

Pause.

Dan   I love her.

Larry   Boo hoo, so do I. You don't love Anna, you love yourself.

Dan   You're wrong, I don't love myself.

Larry   Yes you do, and you know something; you're winning – you selfish people – it's your world. Nice, isn't it?

Dan *glances round the sleek surgery.*

Dan   *Nice* office. She's come back to you because she can't bear your suffering. You don't know who she is, you love her like a dog loves its owner.

Larry   And the owner loves the dog for so doing. Companionship will always triumph over 'passion'.

Dan   You'll hurt her. You'll never forgive her.

Larry   Of course I'll forgive her – I have forgiven her.

Without forgiveness we're savages. You're drowning.

Dan   You only met her because of me.

Larry   Yeah, thanks.

Dan   It's a joke, your marriage to her is a joke.

Larry   I like jokes. Here's a good one ... she never sent the divorce papers to her lawyer.

Pause.

To a towering romantic hero like you I don't doubt I'm somewhat common but I am, nevertheless, what she has chosen. And we must respect what the woman wants. If you go near her again I promise –

The phone rings.

I will kill you.

Larry *picks it up.*

(*Charming.*) Hallo. Uh-huh. OK.

He puts the phone down.

I have patients to see.

Larry *takes his jacket off.*

Dan   When she came here you think she enjoyed it?

Larry   I didn't fuck her to give her a nice time. I fucked her to fuck you up. A good fight is never clean. And yeah, she enjoyed it, she's a Catholic, she loves a guilty fuck.

Larry *grins.*

Dan   You're an animal.

Larry   Yeah and what are you?

Dan   You think love is simple? You think the heart is like a diagram?

Larry   Ever seen a human heart? It looks like a fist wrapped in blood. Go fuck yourself ... you ... WRITER

– You LIAR. Go check a few facts while I get my hands dirty.

Dan   She hates your hands, she hates your simplicity.

Pause.

Larry   Listen, I've spent the last week talking about you.

Beat.

Anna tells me you fucked her with your eyes closed. She tells me you still cry for your mother, you mummy's boy.

Beat.

Shall we stop this?

Beat.

You don't know the first thing about love because you don't understand compromise.

Beat.

You don't even know Alice.

Dan *looks up.*

Larry   Consider her scar, how did she get that?

Dan   When did you see her?

Pause.

Larry   Anna's exhibition. You remember. A scar in the shape of a question mark, solve the mystery.

Dan   She got it when her parents' car crashed.

Larry   When you leave ... doubtless you will notice the beautiful girl in reception. She's my next patient. She has an illness called 'Dermatitis Artefacta'. It's a mental disorder manifested in the skin. The patient manufactures his or her very own skin disease. They pour bleach on themselves, gouge their skin, inject themselves with their own piss, sometimes their own shit. They create their own disease ... with the same diabolical attention to detail as

... the artist ... or the lover.

Beat.

It looks 'real' but its source is the deluded self.

Larry *takes a roll of paper and makes a new sheet on the surgery bed.*

I think Alice mutilated herself. It's fairly common in children who lose their parents young. They blame themselves, they're disturbed.

Dan   Alice is not 'disturbed.'

Larry   But she is. You were so busy feeling your grand artistic 'feelings' you couldn't see what was in front of you. The girl is fragile and tender. She didn't want to be put in a book, she wanted to be loved.

Dan   How do *you* know?

Larry   Clinical observation.

Dan sits, head in hands.

Don't cry on me.

Beat.

Dan   I'm sorry, I don't know what to do ...

Larry   You want my advice? Go back to her.

Dan *(shrugs)*   She'd never have me. She's vanished.

Larry   No she hasn't. I found her ... by accident. She's working in ... a ... 'club'.

Beat.

Yes, I saw her naked. No, I did not fuck her.

Dan   You spoke to her?

Larry   Yes.

Dan   What about?

Larry   You.

The phone rings. **Larry** *picks up the phone.* **Dan** *sees the Newton's Cradle.*

Yes. Yup. One minute.

Larry *puts the phone down. He writes on his prescription pad.*

Dan   How is she?

Larry   She loves you . . . beyond comprehension. Here . . . your prescription. It's where she works. Go to her.

Dan   Thanks.

Pause. **Dan** *points to the Newton's Cradle.*

Where did you get that?

Larry   A present.

Beat. **Larry** *opens his laptop, begins to work.*

Still fucking around on the Net?

Dan   Not recently.

Larry   I liked your book by the way.

Dan   Really?

Larry   I'm not sucking your literary cock but I did quite like it – because it was 'human' (surprisingly) and I'm bored with inhuman things. Anything with a 'cyber' before it I want to kill.

Dan   We met in cyberspace.

Larry   And I wanted to kill you.

Dan   I thought you wanted to fuck me?

Larry   Don't get lippy. You should write another one.

Dan   Haven't got a subject.

Larry   When I was nine a policeman touched me up. He was my uncle – still is . . . Uncle Ted. Nice bloke, married, bit of a demon darts player. Don't tell me you haven't got a subject, every human life is a million stories.

Beat.

Thank God life ends – we'd never survive it.

Beat.

Our flesh is ferocious, our bodies will kill us, our bones will outlive us.

He smiles at **Dan**.

Still writing obituaries?

Dan Yes.

Larry Busy?

Dan Yeah, old people die in the winter.

Larry We're the old people, Dan; old men shaking our fists over these women, like some ancient ritual. We should go back to the aquarium and evolve. From Big Bang to weary shag, the history of the world.

Dan *smiles.*

And if women saw one minute of our home movies, the shit that slops through our minds every day ... they'd string us up by our balls, they really would.

Pause. They look at each other. **Dan** *looks at the Newton's Cradle.*

Dan Alice ... gave me one of those.

Larry Really?

Beat.

Dan And yours?

Larry Oh ... my dad.

Dan Your father?

Larry Yeah, he loves old tat.

Dan He's a cab driver, isn't he?

Larry Yeah.

Larry *points to* **Dan** *indicating, 'and yours'.*

Teacher . . .

Dan History.

Pause. **Larry** *sets the balls on the cradle in motion.*

Larry Strange, isn't it? Everything our parents told us was good for us will kill us . . . sun, milk, meat . . . love. You shouldn't have messed with Anna.

Dan *gets up.*

Dan I know, I'm sorry. Thank you.

Larry For what?

Dan Being nice.

Larry I am nice. Your invoice is in the post.

Dan *goes to exit.*

Larry Dan . . .

Dan *turns.*

Larry I lied to you.

Beat.

I did fuck Alice.

Pause.

Sorry for telling you. I'm just . . . not big enough to forgive you.

Beat.

So go fuck yourself . . . Buster.

Silence. They look at each other.

Blackout.

Scene Eleven

Hotel room.

Late night.

Dan *is lying on the bed, he stubs his cigarette in the ashtray.* **Alice** *is in the bathroom offstage.*

Alice (*off*)   What barks and fucks for England?

Dan   What?

Alice *barks loudly.*

Dan (*laughing*)   It's two in the morning. You'll wake the hotel.

Alice *enters in her stripey pyjamas.*

Alice   Mad dog.

She jumps onto the bed.

Fuck me . . .

Dan   Again? We have to be up at six in the morning.

Alice   How can one man be so endlessly disappointing?

Dan   That's my charm.

Alice *lies in his arms.*

Dan   So . . . where are we going?

Alice   My treat, my holiday surprise, my rules.

Dan *tickles her.*

Dan   Give me a clue.

Alice   New York.

Dan   Really? Great. How long's the flight?

Alice   Seven hours.

Dan   I can't fly for seven hours.

Alice   The plane will do the flying. I'll protect you.

Dan   With what?

Alice   Free booze.

He kisses her.

Dan   Did you remember to pack my passport?

Alice   Of course, your passport is with my passport.

Dan   And where are those passports?

Alice   In a place where you can't look. No one sees my passport photo. Hey, when we get on the plane we'll have been together four years. Happy anniversary, Buster.

Dan   What about . . . the gap?

Alice   (*correcting him*)   Trial separation.

Dan   I'm going to take my eyes out.

Alice   Brush your teeth as well.

Dan   What was in my sandwiches?

Alice   Tuna.

Dan   What colour was my apple?

Alice   Green.

Dan   It was red.

Alice   It was green, I ate it, I know.

Dan   What were your first words to me?

Alice   'Hallo, stranger.' Where had I been?

Dan   Dancing then Smithfield then the buried river.

Alice   The what?

Dan   You went to Blackfriars Bridge to see where the Fleet river comes out, the . . . swimming pig . . . all that.

Alice   You've lost the plot, Grandad.

Dan *exits to the bathroom.*

Dan (*off*) And you went to that park, with the memorial.

Beat.

Alice Who did you go there with?

Dan (*off*) My old dead Dad.

Alice He ate an egg sandwich, he had butter on his chin.

Dan (*off*) How do you remember these things?

Alice Because *my* head's not full of specky egghead rubbish. What was your euphemism?

Dan (*off*) Reserved. Yours?

Alice Disarming. Was your doughnut jam or custard?

Dan enters. *He is wearing glasses now.*

Dan No idea.

Alice Trick question, you had a bun.

Dan *You* are a trick question. Do you remember the doctor?

Alice No . . . what doctor?

Dan There was a doctor. He gave you a cigarette.

Alice No.

Pause.

I haven't been on holiday for . . . ever.

Dan We went to the country . . .

Alice That doesn't count, you were making sneaky calls to that . . . hussy we do not mention.

Beat.

Dan Do you think they're happy?

Alice Who?

Dan Anna and . . . Larry.

Alice   Couldn't give a toss. Kip?

Dan   I want a fag. How did you manage to give up?

Alice   Deep inner strength.

Pause. **Dan** *strokes her leg.*

Dan   How did you get this?

Alice   You know how.

Dan   How?

Alice   I fell off my bike because I refused to use stabilisers.

Dan   Really?

Alice   You know how I got it.

Pause.

Dan   Did you do it yourself?

Alice   No.

Pause.

Dan   Show me your passport.

Alice   No, I look ugly.

Dan   I don't want to see your photo.

Pause.

When are you going to stop stripping?

Alice   Soon.

Dan   You're addicted to it.

Alice   No I'm not. It paid for this.

Beat.

Dan   Tell me what happened...

Alice   Dan ... don't.

Dan   Nothing you say can hurt me, I'm in love with you. You're safe.

Alice Nothing happened.

Dan But he came to the club?

Alice Loads of men came to the club. *You* came to the club. The look on your face.

Dan The look on *your* face. What a face. What a wig. I love your face . . . I saw this face . . . this vision . . . and then you stepped into the road. It was the moment of my life.

Alice *This* is the moment of your life.

Dan You were perfect . . .

Alice I still am.

Dan I know.

Beat.

On the way to the hospital . . . when you were 'lolling' . . . I kissed your forehead.

Alice You brute.

Dan The cabbie saw me kiss you . . . he said 'Is she yours?' and I said 'Yes . . . she's mine.'

He kisses her forehead, holds her close.

So he came to the club, watched you strip, had a little chat and that was it.

Alice Yes.

Dan You're not trusting me. I'm not going to leave you, I'm never going to leave you again. Just tell me so I know. I want to understand you.

Alice You do understand me.

Dan So trust me. If you fucked him you fucked him, I just want to know.

Alice Why?

Dan (*tenderly*)   Because I want to know everything because
... I'm a loony.

Pause.

Tell me ...

Pause.

Alice   Nothing happened. You were living with someone
else.

Dan   What are you justifying?

Alice   I'm not justifying anything ... I'm just saying.

Dan   What are you saying?

Alice   I'm not saying anything. Please don't scare me.

Dan   I just want the truth.

Alice   I'm telling you the truth.

Dan   You and the truth are known strangers. Did you
ever give him a present?

Alice   No, come to bed.

Dan   I'm going for some fags.

Alice   Everywhere's closed.

Dan   I'll go to the terminal. I'll be back soon.

Dan *puts on his coat.*

When I get back please tell me the truth.

Alice   Why?

Dan   Because I'm addicted to it. Because without it we're
animals. Trust me, I love you.

He looks at her.

Dan   What?

Pause.

Alice   I don't love you any more.

Dan   Look . . . I'm sorry . . .

Alice   I've changed the subject, I – don't – love – you – any more.

Dan   Since when?

Alice   Now. Just now. Go please.

She rummages in her rucksack and hands him his passport.

I don't want to lie and I can't tell you the truth so it's over.

Dan   You're leaving me?

Alice   I've left. I've gone. I don't love you any more. Goodbye.

Dan   Why?

Alice   Because I'm bored of loving a piece of shit.

Dan   Why don't you tell me the truth.

Alice   So you can hate me? I fucked Larry, many times, I enjoyed it, I came, I prefer you. Now go.

Pause.

Dan   I knew that. He told me.

Alice   You knew?

Dan   I needed *you* to tell me.

Alice   Why?

Dan   Because he might've been lying. I had to hear it from you.

Alice   I would never have told you because I know you'd never forgive me.

Dan   I would. I have.

Alice   Why did he tell you?

Dan   Because he's a bastard.

Alice   How could he?

Dan   Because he wanted *this* to happen.

Alice   But why test me?

Dan   Because I'm a fucking idiot.

Alice   Yeah, well, I'm bored of loving an idiot. You left me, Dan. You jumped ship. I would've loved you for ever. Now, please go.

Dan   Don't do this, Alice. Talk to me.

Alice   I'm talking, fuck off.

Dan   I'm sorry, you misunderstand, I didn't mean to . . .

Alice   Yes you did.

Dan   I love you.

Alice   Where?

Dan   What?

Alice   Show me. Where is this 'love'? I can't see it, I can't touch it, I can't feel it. I can hear it, I can hear some *words* but I can't do anything with your easy words. So . . . please get out, or I will, which annoys the fuck out of me because this is my treat.

Dan   Listen to me, please . . .

Alice   Whatever you say it's too late.

Dan   Please don't do this . . .

Alice   It's done. Please go or I'll call . . . security.

Dan   You're not in a strip club. There is no security.

She tries to grab the phone. **Dan** *throws her onto the bed. They struggle.*

Alice   What are you going to do now? Beat me up? Rape me? Kill me?

Dan   Why did you fuck him?

Alice I wanted to.

Dan Why?

Alice I desired him.

Dan Why?

Alice You weren't there.

Dan Why him?

Alice He asked me nicely.

Dan You're a liar.

Alice So?

Dan Who the fuck are you?

Alice I'm no one.

Alice *spits in his face. He grabs her by the throat, one hand.*

Go on, hit me. That's what you want. Hit me, you fucker.

Silence.

Dan *hits her.*

Silence.

She stares at him. He looks away.

Alice Do you have a single original thought in your head?

Blackout.

Scene Twelve

Postman's Park.

Afternoon.

A summer's day. **Anna** *is looking at the memorial. She has a guide book.* **Larry** *stands holding his white coat. He carries two styrofoam cups. He watches her. She turns.*

Anna Spy.

Beat.

You've got the coat . . .

Larry   Yes, I have.

Anna   The white coat.

Larry   I'm Larry, the Doctor.

Anna   Hallo, Doctor Larry.

Larry *hands a cup to* **Anna**.

Anna   Thanks. Have you read these?

She wanders back to the memorial. **Larry** *sits on a park bench and lights a cigarette.*

Larry   Yeah, I knew you'd like it.

Anna (*reading*)   Elizabeth Boxall, of Bethnal Green . . . died of injuries received in trying to save a child from a runaway horse. June 20 1888.

Pause.

How's Polly?

Larry   Polly is great.

Anna   I always knew you'd end up with a pretty nurse.

Larry   Yeah? How?

Anna   I just thought you would. Is she . . . 'the one'?

Larry   I don't know . . . no. Everyone learns, nobody changes.

Anna   *You* don't change.

Pause.

Larry   You . . . seeing anyone?

Anna   No. I got a dog.

Larry   Yeah? What sort?

Anna   Mongrel, she's a stray. I found her in the street, no collar, nothing.

Beat.

Actually . . . I'm not seeing anyone but I've got a bit of a date.

Larry Who? I'll kill him.

Anna He's a vet.

Larry See, you can't escape the medics.

Beat.

You look fantastic.

Anna Don't start.

Larry I'd give you one. Serious.

Anna Fuck off and die. You fucked-up slag.

Anna *smiles.*

Larry I never told you this . . . when I strode into the bathroom . . . that night – a bruised colossus, I banged my knee on your cast-iron roll-top trendy tub. The fucking bathroom ambushed me. I was hopping around in agony while you were weeping in the sitting-room. The mirror was having a field day.

Beat.

I hope you'll be thoroughly miserable with your tweedy vet.

Anna I'm sure I will be.

Beat.

Larry How's work?

Anna I'm having a break. I'm taking the dog to my parents, we're going to go for long walks.

Pause.

Larry Don't become . . . a sad person.

Anna I won't. I'm not. Fuck off.

He looks at her.

Larry   Don't give your love to a dog.

Anna   Well, you didn't want it, in the end. There's always someone younger.

Silence. They look out at the memorial.

Larry   How did she die?

Anna   I don't know. All he said was that she died last night in New York. He's flying out today and he wanted to see us before he left.

Larry   So they weren't together?

Anna   No, they split up in January.

Larry   How did they contact him?

Anna   Maybe she wrote his name in her passport as next of kin. You're still in mine, in the event of death. I must remove you.

Pause.

Are you glad you're back here?

Larry   Yeah. Well, Polly refused to have sex with me until I gave up private medicine. What's a man to do?

Pause. **Anna** *reads her guide book, looks up.*

Anna   Who put these here?

Larry   G. F. Watts.

Anna   The artist?

Larry   Yeah, it's the Watts Memorial.

Anna   No, I mean do you think the families arranged them?

Larry   I suppose. It's like putting flowers at the roadside. People need to remember. It makes things seem less . . . random.

Pause.

Actually, I hate this memorial.

Anna   Why?

Larry   It's the sentimental act of a Victorian
philanthropist. We remember the dead and forget the
living.

Anna   You're a pompous bastard.

Beat.

Larry   And you are an incurable romantic.

Pause.

Have a look for Alice Ayres.

Anna   Larry, that's horrible.

Larry *takes the book. He finds the page.*

Larry (*reading*)   'Alice Ayres, daughter of a bricklayer's
labourer, who by intrepid conduct saved three children
from a burning house in Union Street, Borough, at the cost
of her own young life. April 24 1885.'

Pause.

She made herself up.

Anna (*reading*)   'She rescued the three children and then
stood at the window of the burning building . . . "the crowd
implored her to jump . . . dazed and enfeebled she missed
her leap and struck some railings".' She was impaled.

Beat.

'Proposing a national monument to ordinary civilians Watts
sited the example of Alice Ayres . . . "These deeds, happily
far from uncommon, will more than anything constitute in
the far future our claim to be considered a noble people.
The national prosperity of a nation is not an abiding
possession, the deeds of its people are." '

Larry   He was inspired by her . . . the girl in the burning
building . . . romantic death. Was he a good artist?

Anna   Not really.

Larry   I'm not being callous but I've got a lot of patients to see. Give my apologies to Dan. I'm not good at grief.

Anna   You're a coward.

Larry   I know.

Anna (*reading.*)   'Watts wanted other cities to build similar memorials but none did. This is the only one. There are still ninety spaces left.'

Pause.

You do remember me?

They look at each other. **Dan** *enters with a small suitcase (as seen in Scene Five) and a bunch of flowers.*

Dan   I couldn't get away from work, sorry.

Larry   Dan ... I have to ...

Dan   It's fine ...

Pause. They look at each other. **Larry** *exits.*

Dan (*to* **Anna**)   You look well.

Anna   I am well.

Dan *looks out at the memorial.*

Dan   She mentioned this ...

Anna   Dan ...

She gestures for him to sit.

Dan   This is where we sat.

Anna   Who?

Dan   Me and my father, didn't I tell you?

Anna   No, wrong girl, you told Alice ...

Dan   Jane, her name was Jane Jones. The police phoned me, they said someone I knew called Jane had died ... they found her address book. I said there must be a mistake ... they had to describe her ...

There's no one else to identify the body ...

She was knocked down by a car ... on 43rd and Madison.

I don't know if she ...

I went to work today ... I wanted to pretend everything was normal. Graham said, 'Who's on the slab?' I went out by the fire exit and just cried like a baby. I covered my face ... why do we do that?

A man from the Treasury had died. I spent all day writing his obituary.

There's no space. There's not enough space.

The phone rang. It was the police ... they said there's no record of her parents' death ... they said they were trying to trace them ...

Larry was wrong ... the scar ... she fell off her bike.

She said she fell in love with me because I cut off my crusts ... but it was just ... it was only that day ... because the bread broke in my hands ...

Pause.

I bumped into Ruth last week. She's deliriously happy. Married, one kid, another on the way. She married a Spanish poet.

He grimaces.

She translated his work and fell in love with him. Fell in love with a collection of poems. You know what they were called, 'Solitude'.

They laugh. **Dan** *holds on to the flowers.*

I have to put these at Blackfriars Bridge. I have to go, I'll miss the plane.

They stand. They look at each other. Pause.

Bye.

Anna   Yes. Bye.

Dan *and* **Anna** *exit separately.*

Fade.

Appendix to Scene Three

In a production of *Closer* where production budget or
theatre sightlines won't allow for a projected version of this
scene it may be possible for the actors to speak their lines
whilst typing. Permission, in this respect, must be sought
from the author's agent when negotiating the rights for the
production.

The following dialogue may be used:

Scene Three

Early evening.

Dan *is in his flat sitting at a table with a computer. There is a
Newton's Cradle on the table. Writerly sloth, etc.*

Larry *is sitting at his desk with a computer.* **Larry** *is wearing a
white coat.*

They are in separate rooms.

*They speak their 'dialogue' simultaneously to their typing it. The actors
should speak word by word, almost robotically, as if we are hearing
the words coolly appearing on a screen. Thus making a distinction
between 'typed' speech and actual speech (e.g.* **Larry** *on the phone).*

Dan   Hallo.

Larry   Hi.

Dan   Do you come here often?

Larry   Eh?

Dan   Net.

Larry   First time.

Dan   A Virgin. Welcome. What's your name?

Larry   Larry. You?

Beat.

Dan　Anna.

Larry　Nice to meet you.

Pause.

Dan　I love COCK.

Pause.

Larry　You're v. forward.

Dan　This web site is called 'London Fuck'. Do you want sex?

Larry　Yes. Describe you . . .

Dan　30s, dark hair, big mouth . . . epic tits.

Larry　Define epic.

Dan　Thirty-six double D.

Larry　Nice legs?

Dan　Y.

Larry　Because I want to know.

Dan　*smiles.*

Dan　No, 'Y' means 'Yes'.

Larry　Oh.

Dan　I want to suck you senseless.

Larry　Be my guest.

Dan　Wear my wet knickers.

Larry　OK.

Dan　Well hung?

Larry　Nine pounds. (Shit) Nine inches.

Dan　GET IT OUT.

Pause. **Larry** *considers this proposition. The phone on* **Larry**'s *desk rings. Loud. He jumps.*

Larry (*speaking*)   Wait.

Larry (*typing*)   Wait.

Larry *picks up the phone.* **Dan** *lights a cigarette.*

(*Speaking into phone.*) Hallo? What's the histology? Progressive? No, sounds like an atrophy. Bye.

Larry *puts the phone down and goes back to his keyboard.*

Dan *clicks the balls on his Newton's Cradle.*

Larry   Hallo?

Dan *looks at his screen.*

Larry (*speaking*)   Bollocks.

(*Now typing again.*) Anna?

Dan *looks at his screen.*

Larry (*typing*)   ANNA? WHERE ARE YOU?

Dan   Hey, big Larry, what do you wank about?

Larry (*speaking*)   You name it.

Larry   Ex-girlfriends.

Dan   Not current g-friends?

Larry   Never.

Dan   Tell me your sex-ex fantasy.

Larry   Hotel room . . . they tie me up, tease me, won't let me come. They fight over me, six tongues on my cock, balls, perineum, et cetera.

Dan   All hail the Sultan of Twat?

Larry *laughs.*

Larry   Anna, what do you wank about?

Beat. **Dan** *considers.*

Dan   Strangers.

Larry   Details . . .

Dan   They form a queue and I attend to them like a cum hungry bitch, one in each hole and both hands.

Beat.

Larry   Five?

Dan   Mmmm.

Larry*'s phone rings. He picks up the receiver and replaces it without answering. Then takes it off the hook.*

Larry   Then?

Dan   They cum in my mouth arse tits cunt hair.

Larry   (*speaking*)   Jesus.

Larry   (*typing*)   Then?

Dan   I lick it off like the dirty slut I am. Wait, have to type with one hand . . . I'm coming right now . . . oh oh oh oh oh oh oh.

Pause.

Larry   Was it good?

Dan   I'm quivering.

Larry   I'm shocked.

Dan   PARADISE SHOULD BE SHOCKING.

Larry   Are you for real?

Dan   Yes . . . Meet me . . .

Larry   Serious?

Dan   Yes.

Larry   When?

Dan   Now.

Larry   Can't. I'm a doctor. Have to do my rounds.

Dan *laughs*.

Dan   Don't be a pussy. Life without risk is death. Desire, like the world, is an accident. The best sex is anonymous. We live as we dream, ALONE. I'll make you come like a train.

Larry *flicks through his diary*.

Larry   Tomorrow, 1p.m. Where?

Dan   Hackney Marshes.

Larry   Somewhere more central?

Dan   Aquarium, London Zoo.

Larry   1p.m.

Dan   And then a hotel.

Larry   How will I know you?

Dan *thinks*.

Dan   Bring white coat.

Larry   Eh?

Dan   Doctor plus coat equals horn for me.

Larry   OK.

Dan   I send you a rose my love.

Larry   Thanks.

Dan   Bye, Larry, kiss kiss kiss kiss kiss.

Larry   Bye, Anna, kiss kiss kiss kiss kiss kiss kiss.

They look at their screens.

Blackout.

A SELECTED LIST OF
METHUEN MODERN PLAYS

☐ CLOSER	Patrick Marber	£6.99
☐ THE BEAUTY QUEEN OF LEENANE	Martin McDonagh	£6.99
☐ A SKULL IN CONNEMARA	Martin McDonagh	£6.99
☐ THE LONESOME WEST	Martin McDonagh	£6.99
☐ THE CRIPPLE OF INISHMAAN	Martin McDonagh	£6.99
☐ THE STEWARD OF CHRISTENDOM	Sebastian Barry	£6.99
☐ SHOPPING AND F***ING	Mark Ravenhill	£6.99
☐ FAUST (FAUST IS DEAD)	Mark Ravenhill	£5.99
☐ POLYGRAPH	Robert Lepage and Marie Brassard	£6.99
☐ BEAUTIFUL THING	Jonathan Harvey	£6.99
☐ MEMORY OF WATER & FIVE KINDS OF SILENCE	Shelagh Stephenson	£7.99
☐ WISHBONES	Lucinda Coxon	£6.99
☐ BONDAGERS & THE STRAW CHAIR	Sue Glover	£9.99
☐ SOME VOICES & PALE HORSE	Joe Penhall	£7.99
☐ KNIVES IN HENS	David Harrower	£6.99
☐ BOYS' LIFE & SEARCH AND DESTROY	Howard Korder	£8.99
☐ THE LIGHTS	Howard Korder	£6.99
☐ SERVING IT UP & A WEEK WITH TONY	David Eldridge	£8.99
☐ INSIDE TRADING	Malcolm Bradbury	£6.99
☐ MASTERCLASS	Terrence McNally	£5.99
☐ EUROPE & THE ARCHITECT	David Greig	£7.99
☐ BLUE MURDER	Peter Nichols	£7.99
☐ BLASTED & PHAEDRA'S LOVE	Sarah Kane	£7.99

Methuen Contemporary Dramatists
include

Peter Barnes (three volumes)
Sebastian Barry
Edward Bond (six volumes)
Howard Brenton
(two volumes)
Richard Cameron
Jim Cartwright
Caryl Churchill (two volumes)
Sarah Daniels (two volumes)
David Edgar (three volumes)
Dario Fo (two volumes)
Michael Frayn (two volumes)
Peter Handke
Jonathan Harvey
Declan Hughes
Terry Johnson
Bernard-Marie Koltès
Doug Lucie

David Mamet (three volumes)
Anthony Minghella
(two volumes)
Tom Murphy (four volumes)
Phyllis Nagy
Philip Osment
Louise Page
Stephen Poliakoff
(three volumes)
Christina Reid
Philip Ridley
Willy Russell
Ntozake Shange
Sam Shepard (two volumes)
David Storey (three volumes)
Sue Townsend
Michel Vinaver (two volumes)
Michael Wilcox

Methuen World Classics
include

Jean Anouilh (two volumes)
John Arden (two volumes)
Arden & D'Arcy
Brendan Behan
Aphra Behn
Bertolt Brecht (six volumes)
Büchner
Bulgakov
Calderón
Anton Chekhov
Noël Coward (five volumes)
Eduardo De Filippo
Max Frisch
Gorky
Harley Granville Barker
   (two volumes)
Henrik Ibsen (six volumes)
Lorca (three volumes)
Marivaux
Mustapha Matura

David Mercer (two volumes)
Arthur Miller (five volumes)
Molière
Musset
Peter Nichols (two volumes)
Clifford Odets
Joe Orton
A. W. Pinero
Luigi Pirandello
Terence Rattigan
W. Somerset Maugham
   (two volumes)
Wole Soyinka
August Strindberg
   (three volumes)
J. M. Synge
Ramón del Valle-Inclán
Frank Wedekind
Oscar Wilde

Methuen Classical Greek Dramatists

Aeschylus Plays: One
(Persians, Seven Against Thebes, Suppliants,
Prometheus Bound)

Aeschylus Plays: Two
(Oresteia: Agamemnon, Libation-Bearers, Eumenides)

Aristophanes Plays: One
(Acharnians, Knights, Peace, Lysistrata)

Aristophanes Plays: Two
(Wasps, Clouds, Birds, Festival Time, Frogs)

Aristophanes & Menander: New Comedy
(Women in Power, Wealth, The Malcontent,
The Woman from Samos)

Euripides Plays: One
(Medea, The Phoenician Women, Bacchae)

Euripides Plays: Two
(Hecuba, The Women of Troy, Iphigeneia at Aulis,
Cyclops)

Euripides Plays: Three
(Alkestis, Helen, Ion)

Euripides Plays: Four
(Elektra, Orestes, Iphigeneia in Tauris)

Euripides Plays: Five
(Andromache, Herakles' Children, Herakles)

Euripides Plays: Six
(Hippolytos, Suppliants, Rhesos)

Sophocles Plays: One
(Oedipus the King, Oedipus at Colonus, Antigone)

Sophocles Plays: Two
(Ajax, Women of Trachis, Electra, Philoctetes)

Methuen Student Editions

John Arden	*Serjeant Musgrave's Dance*
Alan Ayckbourn	*Confusions*
Aphra Behn	*The Rover*
Edward Bond	*Lear*
Bertolt Brecht	*The Caucasian Chalk Circle*
	Life of Galileo
	Mother Courage and her Children
Anton Chekhov	*The Cherry Orchard*
Caryl Churchill	*Top Girls*
Shelagh Delaney	*A Taste of Honey*
John Galsworthy	*Strife*
Robert Holman	*Across Oka*
Henrik Ibsen	*A Doll's House*
Charlotte Keatley	*My Mother Said I Never Should*
Bernard Kops	*Dreams of Anne Frank*
Federico García Lorca	*Blood Wedding*
John Marston	*The Malcontent*
Willy Russell	*Blood Brothers*
Wole Soyinka	*Death and the King's Horseman*
August Strindberg	*The Father*
J. M. Synge	*The Playboy of the Western World*
Oscar Wilde	*The Importance of Being Earnest*
Tennessee Williams	*A Streetcar Named Desire*
Timberlake Wertenbaker	*Our Country's Good*